High Plains Fandango

Red Shuttleworth

High Plains Fandango

A PLAY

Humanitas Media Publishing

Copyright © 2015. Red Shuttleworth. All Rights Reserved.

CAUTION: This play is fully protected, in whole, in part, or in any form, under the copyright laws of the United States of America, the British Empire including the Dominion of Canada, and all other countries of the copyright union, and are subject to royalty. All rights, including professional, amateur, motion picture, radio, television, recitation, and public reading, are strictly reserved. All inquiries for performance rights should be addressed to the author, Red Shuttleworth (email: redshuttleworth@gmail.com).

ISBN (Print): 978-0-9912037-3-4
ISBN (Kindle): 978-0-9912037-2-7

Cover Photograph by Ed Kashi/VII

Considerable and Special Thanks to Kris Wetherholt for continued faith in my writing and for her work in behalf of publication of *High Plains Fandango*.

For

Maura, Ciara, Luke & Jessi

High Plains Fandango was commissioned in 2010 by the Department of Theatre and Dance, State University of New York, Fredonia.

The author is grateful to the Echo Theater Company (Los Angeles) and to Ethan Phillips for assistance with the development of *High Plains Fandango*. Ethan Phillips directed a public reading of the play at the Zephyr Theatre in Los Angeles on March 14, 2011, with the following cast: Vaughn Armstrong, Gigi Bermingham, Wallace Bruce, Loreni Delgado, Alana Dietze, Steve Hofvendahl, Tara Karsian, Paul Lieber, Rod McLachlan, Annabella Price, Chris Shaw, and Rena Strober.

High Plains Fandango premiered in the Alice E. Bartlett Theatre, Michael C. Rockefeller Arts Center, State University of New York, Fredonia, on February 24, 2012. Produced by the Department of Theatre and Dance, SUNY-Fredonia. The cast was as follows:

    WAITRESS   Kelsey Rispen
    O'GARR   Clayton Howe
    KEN ADAMS   Tony Taylor
    CINTHIA   Cassandra Giovine
    DQ   Claire Elise Walton
    MOSS   Andrew Albigese
    AQUINAS   Jessica Drew-Cates
    FATHER BEN   Nicholas Nieves
    ISABELLE ROCHE   Caitlin Molloy
    LOUIS ROCHE   Sean Marciniak
    JOHN HOOLEY   Jonathan Dimaria

Directed by Tom Loughlin
Scenic Design by Samantha Sayers
Technical Design by Joshua Jansen
Lighting Design by Taylor Morse
Costume Design by Amanda Moore and Josh Porter
Sound Design by Hilda Myer
Production Stage Managed by Elizabeth Voss

High Plains Fandango

Scene One

(*Lights up on a small town café on the eastern edge of the High Plains in western Nebraska.* O'GARR, *jeans, T-shirt, boots, good cowboy hat, is at a table. He is in his late 30's.* WAITRESS, *in her late 30's, wearing a denim skirt, white snap shirt, and apron, walks angry-fast to him, rough-sets a plate of fried eggs onto his table, drops a napkin and clattering silverware in front of him.*)

WAITRESS: It's just a wedding.

O'GARR: At it this early? (*Short pause.*) Not sure I'm hungry. (*Slowly begins to eat.*)

WAITRESS: You go to some cow town school, you pair off. We did that. You go to prom snug in a fake silk, pale gold halter dress, maybe chug a Zoloft with beer. Your boy, drunker 'n a hundred white men loose in Omaha, pukes off a cottonwood in the town square…

O'GARR: Heard all this crap-fantasy before.

WAITRESS: You never heard it once.

O'GARR: Many a once.

WAITRESS: After he pukes, he wants to screw.

O'GARR: You want one more… before my wedding?

WAITRESS: I give him some chewing gum.

O'GARR: You're like an old woman… always telling the same bogus story.

WAITRESS: (*She lifts her skirt to her upper thighs for a moment.*) This ain't old lady flesh, O'Garr.

O'GARR: Bring some juice, would you?

WAITRESS: Choke. (*Pause.*) It's just a wedding… and they don't matter… not to stud ranchers. (*Pause.*) When the new wears off, you'll come begging for old times.

O'GARR: Try being happy for me.

WAITRESS: Like you'd be happy for me.

O'GARR: Yep.

WAITRESS: Ain't you the one who said you'd kill any man who even looked at me?

O'GARR: I was seventeen.

WAITRESS: You were in love. (*Pause.*) So I was wrong… to believe in you.

O'GARR: Most beliefs come 'n go. Not to mention the fact that believers can be bought.

WAITRESS: I hope your bride gives you dick-drippin' syphilis.

O'GARR: Bat Masterson said it first. "Believers can be bought." He was speaking of New York politicians… how there's a patronage system in politics.

WAITRESS: What does Bat fucking Masterson have to do with you and me and you bringing some suburban Lincoln girl out here to marry you?

O'GARR: Don't let your brain injure your pleasures.

WAITRESS: I think we share a lot more than pleasure.

O'GARR: We don't share the *Stockman's Weekly*. We don't share breaking stock tank ice in winter.

WAITRESS: That again.

O'GARR: You were asked.

WAITRESS: I was asked what?

O'GARR: Ranch life.

WAITRESS: With no guarantees. (*Pause.*) I had to keep this café running. Mom was already failing.

O'GARR: You had first offer.

WAITRESS: With no mention of marriage.

O'GARR: Some stuff don't have to be said.

(KEN, *a trim military-looking man in his late 30's, dressed corporate-casual, enters with a slight limp. O'GARR and WAITRESS give KEN a glance of dismissal, then return to their talk. KEN finds a menu, takes in the situation, chooses a table to sit at, and essentially becomes the fly-on-the-wall.*)

WAITRESS: But you proposed to her. It was in the newspaper. Kind of a surprise. You go down to Lincoln for a college reunion. When you get back, it's in the paper. (*Pause.*) You show up at her condo a'horseback… with a goddamned guitar… and you propose? Tarted-up like Roy fucking Rogers… and you propose?

O'GARR: She's prone to that sort of gesture. You ain't. You would a laughed.

WAITRESS: I'm laughing good right now. But don't think we're going on, not you and me.

O'GARR: I don't want you feeling left out.

(WAITRESS *picks up his plate and slams it off his head.*
O'GARR *falls off his chair, sprawls on the floor, sits, slowly stands.*)

O'GARR: Entertain' what-all comes with breakfast here. (*He returns to his seat.*)

WAITRESS: You're a walking hardness. That's your problem. You follow your hardness.

O'GARR: Let's go in the back.

WAITRESS: You gonna send her back to Lincoln?

O'GARR: Don't make this complicated.

WAITRESS: I am not your bachelor party, buster.

O'GARR: Half my egg is on the floor and you ain't brought me something to drink. Can we make it personal pleasure or breakfast?

(CINTHIA, *late 20's to early 30's, enters. She is in khaki shorts and a pullover blouse.*)

O'GARR: Good morning, Cinthia.

WAITRESS: (To CINTHIA) Want a menu?

(CINTHIA *goes to* O'GARR, *hand to his chest.*)

O'GARR: Didn't want to wake you.

WAITRESS: Make a choice, lady… menu or no menu.

O'GARR: (*To* WAITRESS.) This here's Cinthia. She's gonna be my…

WAITRESS: …wife. Congratulations. Just call me Waitress.

CINTHIA: Waitress?

WAITRESS: I was born a Mary, but I'm a waitress, so call me that.

CINTHIA: Mary's a nice name.

O'GARR: We gotta git.

WAITRESS: You showed up way too late to call me Mary. (*To* O'GARR.) You gonna pay your bill or just stroll out?

O'GARR: Put it on my tab.

WAITRESS: Your tab's run out.

CINTHIA: This town is so swell… like a hidden, secret, romantic place. Waitress, I hope we can be close friends.

WAITRESS: This town is nine kinds of hell when blizzards blow in. Nine kinds of hell when there's drought. That's eighteen kinds of regular hell. You don't appear to know even one kind of hell… not yet.

O'GARR: (*Arm around* CINTHIA.) Gotta git.

(O'GARR *and* CINTHIA *step from the café, which dims.*)

CINTHIA: She's a strange one.

O'GARR: She's okay.

CINTHIA: Don't tell me you two have a history. (*She kisses him.*)

Scene Two

(MOSS *and* DQ *are rural small town high school kids.* MOSS *is a town kid and looks it... apparently fated to leave after graduation and never return.* DQ *is in well-worn cut-off jeans, a short-sleeved Western shirt, distressed jogging shoes.*)

MOSS: Wait here. No screwin' off.

DQ: Steal some beer from Hooley's.

MOSS: No beer.

DQ: Beer!

MOSS: Hooley'd hunt us with a bullwhip. (*Pause.*) A couple of Cokes.

DQ: No balls. Moss has no balls. (*Louder.*) Moss has no balls!

(MOSS *slaps* DQ.)

DQ: Didn't hurt.

MOSS: Don't talk to tourists. And stay here.

DQ: Beer! Show some balls. (*As* MOSS *exits*.) I don't want Coke, Moss!

(FATHER BEN, *all black polyester, enters*.)

FATHER BEN: How's DQ today?

DQ: If you're goin' to Hooley's, tell Moss to hurry up. I'm broilin' out here. (*As* FATHER BEN *starts walking away*). Hey!

FATHER BEN: You certainly are into the oats this fine day.

DQ: Talk to me.

FATHER BEN: Yes?

DQ: The archbishop send you here to dry out… or were you screwin' lonesome widows?

FATHER BEN: You already know.

DQ: At least you ain't Chester-the-Molester.

FATHER BEN: We all sin. I… I am praying for forgiveness.

DQ: Don't pray too hard. You'd be better off with a secret girlfriend.

FATHER BEN: That's the last thing I want.

DQ: You're too fuckin' creepy as a goody-goody.

FATHER BEN: And we all have trials.

DQ: Like me being a ward of this town.

FATHER BEN: Is it a trial, really? We don't mean it to be.

DQ: Everyone pitches in, sure. But that doesn't mask that my parents just drove off without me… no warning.

FATHER BEN: (*Gives* DQ *an awkward hug.*) Take no shame, DQ. Take pride.

DQ: "Pride before the fall."

FATHER BEN: No… like pride in being loved by others… and, in your case, being loved by choice.

DQ: Right. I should rise against self-pity.

(MOSS *enters with two 20-ounce bottles of water. He hands one to* DQ.)

DQ: No beer? You're scared of ol' Hooley, you cunny-drip.

FATHER BEN: DQ, please control your language! (*He exits.*)

MOSS: Drink the water. Hooley smacked my head, then made me buy 'em. You drink it.

(MOSS *and* DQ *take long drinks from their bottles.*)

Scene Three

(*In the office of the Roche Motel,* LOUIE *and* ISABELLE, *a married couple in their forties or early fifties, are bickering. It is a cheap, cinderblock and clapboard, ill-insulated, mouse-chawed motel.* LOUIE *is in a non-reenactment-quality outfit meant to resemble what Wyatt Earp wore in Dodge City and Tombstone.* ISABELLE *is dressed up as Calamity Jane.*)

ISABELLE: Calamity Jane would never, not ever, thank any man for coming to her rescue. She was a proto-feminist.

LOUIE: She wasn't proto-anything. She was bi.

ISABELLE: Bi is bullshit.

LOUIE: You saw it on *Deadwood*, just like me.

ISABELLE: That's TV, not history.

LOUIE: It was history made for TV.

ISABELLE: I am not making a point about TV. I am talking about me, me as Calamity Jane. And you as Wyatt Earp.

LOUIE: I run in… as Wyatt Earp. You, as Calamity Jane, have just been saved from perverted desperados. So you're grateful.

ISABELLE: I have to be, as Calamity Jane, drunk. Filthy drunk. Filthy, slept in my own pissy clothes, stinky drunk. And not grateful. How can I be grateful to Wyatt Earp for saving me if I'm hung over and still half pissy drunk? Makes no sense.

LOUIE: Just let me run in… and then you say, "Oh, Marshal Earp, you saved me."

ISABELLE: It's a stupid thing for Calamity Jane to say.

LOUIE: (*Pause.*) Okay, what is it then, Miss Calamity Jane, that you do wish to say?

ISABELLE: How about, "What are you doing here, faggot?"

LOUIE: Ridiculous and wrong.

ISABELLE: Ridiculous and wrong? How about naming this the Roche Motel when we bought it on the settlement money? Who wants to stay at a Roche Motel?

LOUIE: We named it the Roche Motel, R-O-C-H-E Motel, because that is my name. And it's your name. I am Louie Roche. You are Isabelle Roche.

ISABELLE: You don't name a motel after a common, despised household pest. What if our names were R-A-T-T? Would this be the Ratt Motel? Roche Motel is as ridiculous as me, Calamity Jane, being rescued by Wyatt Earp. (*Brief Pause.*) Go on outside and then rush in. We'll try it your way.

(LOUIE *exits. ISABELLE stares up, scratches where it itches, as if getting into character. LOUIE enters at a jog.*)

LOUIE: I forgot my gun.

ISABELLE: Then you ain't much use to me, pard.

LOUIE: Isabelle, where are the guns?

ISABELLE: (*Picks up the office stapler, hands it to him.*) Use this.

LOUIE: This is not a gun.

(LOUIE *exits after setting down the stapler. ISABELLE lifts her fake leather skirt and scratches as if she has crabs, then laughs.*)

ISABELLE: Roche Motel! The one and only Roche Motel on the High Plains. (*Pause.*) The Crabs Motel. The Louse Motel. The Stinkbug Motel. Motel Fire Ant. Motel Viagra. Motel Syphilis. The Spasm Arms. The Crotch Rot Garden Motel… Free Old West Reenactments and a Continental Breakfast of Greenish Grizzly Bear Bacon.

(LOUIE *enters with a wooden pistol and a rough-crafted wooden rifle. He hands the rifle to* ISABELLE.)

ISABELLE: Let's just start from here. No need to run outside.

LOUIE: (*Establishes a manly, Western pose.*) You okay, Miss Calamity?

ISABELLE: Oh, Wyatt, thank god you're here. Who knows what could have happened? I have every venereal disease known to man, plus raging consumption, which shall one day be known as tuberculosis.

LOUIE: (*Pause.*) At the risk of tampering with perfection, Isabelle, can we take it from the top again… with some sincerity?

ISABELLE: Louie, we should fix this place up. Wallpaper. A paint job. Get a loan for the roof. Fill in the parking lot pavement cracks. Put a pool out back.

LOUIE: Stop that. We're gonna sell this motel… at a profit. Watch 'n see.

ISABELLE: We can start with small repairs. And a name change… to something romantic. (*Pause.*) By October we'll be broke.

LOUIE: Let me deal with the finances. Do you or do you not want to be Calamity Jane today?

ISABELLE: Oh, Wyatt, baby, just rip my rags off me.

LOUIE: Isabelle, we have to build up to that part.

(MOSS *enters, takes in the costumed couple.*)

MOSS: Nice afternoon, Mr. and Mrs. Roche.

LOUIE: Can't you see we're trying to run a business

MOSS: That's why I came inside.

LOUIE: You got the weekly rent for DQ?

MOSS: Father Ben is gonna bring it by as soon as the mayor writes the check.

ISABELLE: Moss, how'd you like a summer job, helping us fix the motel up?

LOUIE: Sorry, Moss, ain't no summer work to be had.

MOSS: Your soda pop machine is busted again.

LOUIE: Go to Hooley's.

ISABELLE: Louie, that bastard charges half a dollar more for a Coke.

LOUIE: So what am I supposed to do? The Coke driver comes on Tuesdays. Today is Friday.

ISABELLE: That's what I've been talking about. We have to start doing some upkeep and repairs.

MOSS: I'm just a bit thirsty, that's all.

ISABELLE: Let me find a dollar, Moss. You go to Hooley's. (ISABELLE *goes to a cash box, fishes out a dollar bill, hands it to* MOSS.)

LOUIE: (*As* MOSS *accepts the dollar and turns to leave.*) Kid, you want to help us with an Old West reenactment we're doing?

ISABELLE: Louie, Moss is thirsty.

LOUIE: Heritage is important, Moss. You learn things in reenactments that they fail to teach in school. (*Pause.*) See:

I'm Wyatt Earp. And Mrs. Roche is Calamity Jane. Wyatt Earp rushes into the saloon in Dodge City…

ISABELLE: Deadwood.

LOUIE: …to rescue her from villains. Or villain. (*Hands* MOSS *the stapler.*) Pretend this is a Colt .45. We're out of guns for now.

MOSS: Uh huh.

ISABELLE: Moss, you don't have to do this. Just go to Hooley's for a Coke.

LOUIE: Moss wants to do this… wants to learn his Western heritage. Right, Moss?

MOSS: Guess it'll be something new.

LOUIE: It'll place you one step ahead of your school teachers this fall. (LOUIE *positions* MOSS *behind* ISABELLE *with the stapler to her neck.*) Good. You hold that position, Moss, until I run in. We'll grapple for the pistol in your hand. It'll be just like… like high school wrestling. We do still have wrestling at the school, don't we?

MOSS: Wrestling doesn't interest me much.

LOUIE: Give it your best, kid.

ISABELLE: I wish I was the one going to Hooley's for an over-priced Coke. (LOUIE *exits.* ISABELLE *wraps* MOSS' *free arm around her waist, leans back into him.*) I won't let him hurt you.

MOSS: Appreciate it.

(LOUIE *enters, melodramatically pauses.*)

LOUIE: You okay, Miss Calamity?

ISABELLE: Oh, Wyatt, thank god you're here.

(LOUIE *rushes at them, spins them, wrestles for the stapler.* MOSS *trips* LOUIE, *drops him quickly to the floor.*)

LOUIE: (*Yelps in pain.*) Fuck, fuck, fuck. (*Pause.*) My fucking back is wrenched!

(ISABELLE *goes to the cash box, brings back a couple of dollars, hands them to* MOSS.)

ISABELLE: Get an extra Coke. Give a bottle to DQ. Tell her the hazards there were in the old wild West.

Scene Four

(*In the church graveyard, a few stones nearby like old crooked teeth, KEN sits on a park bench, legs outstretched. KEN is in khaki trousers, sports coat, and tie. His hair is cut into a military high-and-tight. After a few beats, AQUINAS, a woman in her mid-twenties, enters holding a bouquet of flowers. She is in a below-the-knees, buttoned-to-the-throat conservative dress, and her long hair is pulled up into a bun. AQUINAS does not notice KEN.*)

KEN: (*After a moment.*) Hello.

AQUINAS: (*Startled.*) Goodness! You surprised me.

KEN: I'm sorry.

AQUINAS: Usually it's just me.

KEN: With flowers.

AQUINAS: (*She looks at the flowers in her hand.*) It's.... I startle easy. (*Pause.*) You're the new man... who lives in the missile silo.

KEN: Ken. Ken Adams. I bought some canned goods from you at the store. Hooley's.

AQUINAS: Yes. I'm Aquinas.

(AQUINAS *looks down for a moment.* KEN *stares into the distance.* AQUINAS *moves to a grave, sets the flowers down, keeps her jaw down briefly, turns toward* KEN.)

AQUINAS: Glad to meet you. You might stop in with us more often. (*Pause.*) We have specials on Wednesdays.

KEN: I'll keep that in mind.

AQUINAS: That's the morning for fresh produce. Seasonal of course. (*She turns as if to leave.*)

KEN: Excuse me. (*Brief pause as* AQUINAS *turns to face him.*) It occurs to me… would you like to have dinner some night? See a movie?

AQUINAS: What?

KEN: A movie and dinner.

AQUINAS: I can't. I'm Aquinas Hooley… as in Mrs. Hooley.

KEN: Oh no, I thought he was your father.

AQUINAS: My father.

KEN: Yes. I thought you… you might be available.

AQUINAS: Available. No. I'm Hooley's wife.

KEN: Forgive me. (*Pause.*) If you weren't Mrs. Hooley, would you accept a dinner and movie date?

AQUINAS: Accept?

KEN: Would you?

AQUINAS: But I am married.

KEN: And you just wanted to place flowers on the grave of a loved one…

AQUINAS: Loved one? (*Pause.*) No, they're not kin of mine. (*Pause.*) I place flowers on graves, the older graves, where no one pays attention anymore.

KEN: You're a nice person, Aquinas.

AQUINAS: You seem nice, too.

KEN: And you're beautiful. (*Pause as* AQUINAS *fidgets, looks down.*) So it was natural for me to ask.

AQUINAS: We don't have movies in this town. The café closes most afternoons at three. Though we sell sandwiches at our store. Fresh made sandwiches. We sell them after three.

KEN: There's a movie house in Valentine and another in Chadron. Both those towns have restaurants.

AQUINAS: But I'm married.

KEN: My mistake, because I'm new to the area.

AQUINAS: In the missile silo.

KEN: Yes… and new to the missile silo. (*Pause.*) But that doesn't change that you're beautiful. Hooley is a lucky man.

AQUINAS: Lucky. John Hooley is good.

KEN: He must be to have courted and won your hand.

AQUINAS: (*Pause as she studies him.*) Why did you buy the silo?

KEN: It was cheap. (*Pause.*) Would you like to visit the silo?

AQUINAS: I can't

KEN: With Mr. Hooley.

AQUINAS: He would say it's foolishness.

KEN: Visiting a newcomer… one who doesn't shop with him often?

AQUINAS: No, just foolishness. (*Pause.*) You have the silo and the forty acres around it.

KEN: You should see it. It was part of our nation's defense during the Cold War.

AQUINAS: But they took the atom bomb away and left it empty.

KEN: Not too empty. They left behind some standard issue furniture. A few couches, sofas. And the commanding officer's quarters are almost luxurious. Nice place. Cool in summer. Inexpensive to heat in winter, though I haven't seen the first snow fly yet.

AQUINAS: It's been nice to meet you, Mr. Adams.

KEN: Ken. Call me Ken. (*He stands, offers his hand.*)

AQUINAS: (*Slowly accepts his hand… as if afraid of being tricked.*) Please consider giving us your business.

KEN: You should never refuse a compliment. Or shy from it.

AQUINAS: (*Gently pulls back… without success.*) Mr. Hooley is waiting at the store.

KEN: Why dodge a truth? Sometimes a compliment is a truth. Just an innocent flat-stated truth. (*Pause.*) As in… you are a beautiful young woman, Aquinas.

AQUINAS: (*Her hand released, she starts to leave.*) Mr. Hooley says, "Beauty is as beauty does."

KEN: Yes. But finally, Aquinas, beauty always does. Beauty is always doing… or it withers.

AQUINAS: (*Walking backwards, waving tentatively.*) Mr. Hooley is waiting.

KEN: You should unbutton the top button of your dress, Aquinas. Breathe, Aquinas, breathe.

(AQUINAS *trips, falls backwards.* KEN *rushes, stiff-legged, limp pronounced, and assists her up.*)

Scene Five

(*In front of Hooley's general store,* HOOLEY, *a man in his late fifties or even sixty, in black trousers and a blue polo shirt, has his head down, his hands on his knees, and is breathing heavily. Sheets of paper are at his feet. Each sheet proclaims, "Always High Prices."* MOSS *and* DQ *are darting at* HOOLEY, *smacking him with placard sticks.*)

MOSS: (*Shouts.*) Get five dollar Cokes at Hooley's. Today's Special: higher prices than ever!

DQ: Boycott Hooley!!!

HOOLEY: Little maggots.

MOSS: We're gonna break you, Hooley.

(MOSS *and* DQ *whack* HOOLEY, *who lurches, throws an awkward punch into nowhere.*)

HOOLEY: You two weren't born. You're spillage from a urinal! (*He charges* MOSS *and* DQ, *slips and falls.*)

DQ: Don't look puzzled, Hooley. Your day was coming.

MOSS: Today's your day, Hooley! (*Pause.*) Two-dollar bottles of water. What kind of shit is that? We live on top of a fresh water ocean!

DQ: Wal-Mart's gonna eat you up!

HOOLEY: Wal-Mart in a county down to less than a thousand souls? You want Wal-Mart, get some fool to drive you to North Platte. That's your best hope. A life working for Wal-Mart.

(AQUINAS *enters, the top button of her dress now unbuttoned. She looks at the others and they look at her.*)

HOOLEY: Call the sheriff, Aquinas.

DQ: For what, Hooley? You want the sheriff to arrest you?

MOSS: Assault on a minor. What's that worth, DQ?

HOOLEY: Call the sheriff! Look what the little bastards did. (*Pause.*) Here, on the pavement.

AQUINAS: The pavement, here? (*She looks down and around.*)

HOOLEY: The papers. Look at the papers, Aquinas. (*Weary, he picks up a couple sheets of paper.*) They taped slogans all over the store. (*Pause.*) Vandalism. Legally speaking, that's vandalism. People go to prison for less. (*Waves a couple sheets of paper.*)

MOSS: You hit a minor. Assault of a minor.

DQ: Hooley, you're going to prison. High prices lead to prison.

AQUINAS: John, we should go into the store.

HOOLEY: I want this settled.

(FATHER BEN *enters.*)

FATHER BEN: A ruckus on a Sunday… on the Lord's day?

HOOLEY: There is no Lord, you idiot soul scrubber. (*Pause.*) Go find another widow woman to jerk you off. Leave us be.

DQ: (*To* FATHER BEN) What's a fair price for a 20-ounce bottle of water?

MOSS: Or a roll of toilet paper? Or a pound of rancid burger? What's a fair price for that?

HOOLEY: Father Ben, I am going to do the reasonable thing. The thing a man in my situation should do. I am going back into my store…

FATHER BEN: Good, Hooley. The right thing for a Sunday.

HOOLEY: … back into my store… and then I am coming back out here with a shotgun. (*Pauses for breath.*) So if you don't get Moss and DQ away out of here, it's going to get real Western real quick.

(FATHER BEN, *like a sheepdog, moves* MOSS *and* DQ *away… and they exit.*)

HOOLEY: (*Looks at* AQUINAS.) Your top button's come undone. You appear immodest.

AQUINAS: I was warm in church.

HOOLEY: You're no longer in church. Button up.

AQUINAS: I remain warm.

HOOLEY: Button up, damn it!

AQUINAS: (*Buttons the top button of her dress.*) John, am I beautiful?

HOOLEY: Stop blathering.

AQUINAS: Do you find me beautiful?

HOOLEY: (*Looks at her as if seeking a symptom.*) What manner of question is that?

AQUINAS: So I am not beautiful?

HOOLEY: (*Pause.*) You have some beauty, yes. But beauty is as beauty does.

AQUINAS: John, what does beauty do?

(*They exit into the store.*)

Scene Six

(*Night... O'GARR's home office. O'GARR, in jeans and a clean T-shirt, is in a wooden swivel chair near a simple hardwood desk with a ledger on it. Photographs of cattle are on the walls. LOUIE, dressed in trousers, dress shirt, and tie, is sitting forward on a sofa.*)

LOUIE: I wouldn't be talking to you if I hadn't meditated on all this.

O'GARR: You meditated?

LOUIE: This is vital to the future.

O'GARR: I don't have time for it.

LOUIE: You don't have time for the future?

O'GARR: Meditation.

LOUIE: All great men meditate. (*Pause.*) The project, O'Garr, the project.

O'GARR: There's no objective correlative.

LOUIE: Objective correlative?

O'GARR: To meditation. Nobody's there when you meditate, right?

LOUIE: Well, yes. It's meant to be a solitary activity.

O'GARR: So it's the same as jacking off.

LOUIE: Jacking off?

O'GARR: Yeah, Louie. Jacking off and your meditation, it's basically the same, because it doesn't involve anybody.

LOUIE: (*Pause.*) The project will involve everybody.

O'GARR: Everybody? Like a dictatorship?

(CINTHIA *enters. She is in an expensive two-piece swimsuit… and holds a bulging 10 x 13 manila envelope. She is taken aback by* LOUIE's *presence.*)

O'GARR: Hi, Cin. You know Louie Roche. Roche Motel and all.

LOUIE: (*Looks down.*) Hello, Mrs. O'Garr.

CINTHIA: (*Holds the envelope in front of herself.*) How's the motel, Louie?

LOUIE: It's been a slow summer. That DQ is a hellion. And the Coke machine's been on and off the blink. Just last week some fellow from Omaha got sick and puked his room. It wasn't as bad as that suicide guy last autumn. Shotgun made a mess of his head. Poor business climate. And the cost of doing laundry… sheets and pillowcases…

O'GARR: What Louie means, Cin, is we're about done talking. He's gotta go meditate.

CINTHIA: You should stop by more often, Louie, and bring along Isabelle. We can all meditate together.

LOUIE: (*To* O'GARR.) So are you gonna sign up for the town's development committee?

O'GARR: And bring in factories?

LOUIE: Not big ones. I was thinking a few small manufacturers… offer them free dilapidated property… falling-down homes. We can transform this town… this county.

O'GARR: And build a big jail for all the illegals we'll have to arrest?

LOUIE: Illegals? That won't happen here. But what will happen, if the average age of our county population keeps climbing, what will happen is we'll just blow away. We have to have jobs to keep our young here. We are suffering from youth drain… brain drain.

O'GARR: Yep… a lot of brains draining in this county.

LOUIE: And we can draw tourists in with events… like an Old West Days festival… with gunfighter reenactments. Fast draw competitions. Stage coach robberies. Buffalo burger cook-offs. We could have a parade with some a those Indians from up on the Rez.

O'GARR: Use your brights, Louie.

LOUIE: My brights?

O'GARR: When you leave, drive slow and use your brights.

(LOUIE *exits with a wave. O'GARR picks up the ledger on his desk, opens it, grabs a pen and starts to write, and stops.*)

O'GARR: Cin, what do you make of that new guy… the one in the missile silo?

CINTHIA: Not much… just a veteran I hear. Afghanistan. Some place like that.

O'GARR: He's been putting a whole lot of mileage on his rig.

CINTHIA: This town *is* pretty far from everything.

O'GARR: The miles he drives are in-county. He's got some angle. Ol' slicks like him are trouble.

CINTHIA: I've got angles… beautiful body angles. Want to play? (*As* O'GARR *takes off his T-shirt,* CINTHIA *steps back.*) First… can we talk?

O'GARR: Not again, Cin. You've got to stop tryin' to work me.

CINTHIA: Are we going to honeymoon or not?

O'GARR: The county newspaper, the Lincoln paper… they both said that Mr. and Mrs. O'Garr were going to honeymoon on his ranch.

CINTHIA: I want to go somewhere… some romantic place.

O'GARR: This place is pretty romantic. Miles of privacy.

CINTHIA: Baby… you're right. I'm sorry. This is beautiful… just like I imagined. And you're all you appeared to be that night in Lincoln… honest-rugged, not a dress-up cowboy, but a guy who…. Well, O'Garr, you just swept me off a ledge. No flowers or fake gestures. None of that "I'll change the diapers when we have kids" weak-tea dribble. (*Pause.*) You're just a wild horse I like to ride. (*Pause.*) But there is the problem, lover, of no swimming pool. And do not suggest driving up to the Niobrara River again.

O'GARR: Boy I went to school with here, Donny Ghosthorse, he told me one time that Crazy Horse performed more and better miracles than Jesus.

CINTHIA: I hate history.

O'GARR: One time in school, Donny says to me, "Your Jesus walked on water, sure. But Crazy Horse rode his pony on top of the Niobrara. So what's the bigger miracle, a 120-pound Jew boy walking on water, or a Lakota warrior on a horse riding on it?"

CINTHIA: We can afford to put in a swimming pool.

O'GARR: I start putting in swimming pools and not buyin' a couple replacement bulls… then I'll lose this place.

CINTHIA: What's the point of me ordering a new swimsuit if there's no place to swim? (*Pause.*) Sweetheart… let's not argue. I love you so much. (*Pause.*) Please. There's travel brochures in this envelope. All we gotta do is pick one destination. Just take a week off. To be together.

O'GARR: We are together, Cin. But it ain't a good together if you're tormenting me over a splurge we can't afford.

CINTHIA: Can't afford. We own twenty-three sections of land. Own. You don't have a mortgage. (*Pouts…. Pause.*) Okay… fine! Then let my mom and dad pay for it.

O'GARR: That's not our way. We don't ask anybody for help.

CINTHIA: You love me?

O'GARR: That's what I'd like to demonstrate… somewhere close by… real personal-like.

CINTHIA: (*Picks up his ledger.*) Get personal with your cow ledger!

(CINTHIA *flips the ledger at* O'GARR *and exits.*)

Scene Seven

(*The café.* MOSS *and* DQ *are finishing a basket of fries and milk shakes.* WAITRESS *brings a cheeseburger to* KEN *--dressed in shorts, T-shirt, athletic shoes-- and drops the plate from a height of about an inch.* MOSS *and* DQ *turn and look.* KEN *does not react.* WAITRESS *brings him a plastic ketchup container, slams it down in front of him, walks away.*)

MOSS: Waitress, guess who's splashin' herself these days with strawberry-stinky perfume?

WAITRESS: Don't get me into something, Moss.

MOSS: Lollipop strawberry perfume.

DQ: Shut up.

WAITRESS: Kids, I ain't in the mood.

(MOSS *and* DQ *stand, pick up their shakes, and start to exit, but stop in front of* KEN.)

MOSS: How's she goin' today, Mr. Silo Man?

KEN: (*Looks up from the cheeseburger he's started to eat.*) You kids ought to visit. It's cool.

(MOSS *and* DQ *snicker, laugh, and exit.*)

KEN: Kids. You have to love 'em.

WAITRESS: Screw yourself. (*She cleans up after the kids.*)

KEN: All I said was, "Kids. You have to love 'em."

WAITRESS: Just who the fuck are you, Mr. Ken Adams… and what are you doing in my town?

KEN: (*Pause.*) I'm just a guy who's retired… found an inexpensive place to live.

WAITRESS: Inexpensive? Last time you're in here, you leave a forty-dollar tip for a six-buck sandwich and iced tea.

KEN: That offend you?

WAITRESS: Sends up red flags. Largest tip in this café's fifty-year history.

KEN: Two twenties is the largest tip?

WAITRESS: What were you hopin' to buy for forty dollars?

KEN: Just paying proper respect for your service.

WAITRESS: Finish eating and get out. And don't come back.

KEN: *(Pause as he takes a bite of his cheeseburger.)* Aren't you being unkind?

WAITRESS: The word is wary. I'm being wary.

KEN: Ask any question you want about me… I'll give you straight answers.

WAITRESS: When you were a banker, lawyer, or some other kind of thief, how much money did you swindle?

KEN: Lawyer? I was too antsy in a classroom to become a lawyer. I barely graduated from West Point. Military Academy. *(Pause… holds up a hand.)* Brief career. Took two Taliban rounds to my leg. Lucky I still have the leg. *(Points to the leg brace on a scarred leg.)* So I'm retired.

WAITRESS: That tip painted you bogus! *(Pause.)* Unless you figured it'd make my pussy wet.

KEN: I have no ulterior motives.

WAITRESS: So I ain't the kind of woman you'd want in bed. Great. You insult everybody?

KEN: I don't want to fight. I was just being sincere.

WAITRESS: I know all about sincere.

KEN: You're attacking me for no fathomable reason.

WAITRESS: So, Mr. Career Army, what did they teach you to do in this sort of case?

KEN: (*Pause.*) I'm supposed to ask you out.

WAITRESS: You are nuts… a fucking crazed weasel.

KEN: Why? Because you're a beautiful woman? Is it wrong for a guy to…

WAITRESS: …to try to buy pussy with a forty dollar tip?

KEN: Then the offer is off the table.

WAITRESS: What a fucking relief.

KEN: How about a movie in Valentine?

WAITRESS: I'm busy.

KEN: And you're bitter.

WAITRESS: You got no right to judge me… or guess me… or make up my emotional state to suit your motives!

KEN: Okay… to make this right, you pay for the gas and for the movie.

WAITRESS: What?

KEN: This way we can start all over… get to know each other.

WAITRESS: Hmmmmm… You. Are. Cute.

(WAITRESS *slinks sensually to* KEN. *She picks up the ketchup container as she bends to apparently kiss him… and douses his shirt with ketchup.*)

Scene Eight

(*Inside Hooley's General Store,* HOOLEY *and* AQUINAS *are in front of a largely unsupplied display case. Three cardboard boxes are on the floor.* HOOLEY *is in a grocer's smock worn over a dress shirt and trousers.* AQUINAS *is wearing a white collared blouse, the top two buttons undone, and a pleated, parochial school style skirt that falls well below her knees. Her hair is up.*)

HOOLEY   (*Takes a cookie package from a box, holds it up.*) These are brand new, just baked apricot/raspberry Verona cookies.

AQUINAS: They're very nice.

HOOLEY: I hope you haven't been eating the profits, Aquinas. (*Pause. He waits as she bows her head.*) So we take some fresh packages… and we place them at the rear of the display. (*Pause.*) Then we, from that point, place our out-of-date packages in front of them until we have just two rows left to do.

AQUINAS: Why are we selling out-of-date cookies?

HOOLEY: Because, Aquinas, they're not truly expired.

AQUINAS: They're not?

HOOLEY: They are stamped with a foolish sell-by-this-date stamp... thanks to over-regulation.

AQUINAS: Isn't this against the law?

HOOLEY: Aquinas, you are not following me. (*Pause.*) Okay... with two rows left, we integrate the two kinds of dates. Half and half. (*Pause.*) You have three big boxes to work from. A box of fresh cookie packages... and two boxes of older cookie packages to mix in with them.

AQUINAS: And it's a sale? On apricot/raspberry cookies that are now against the law to sell?

HOOLEY: The cookies, if you taste them, are the same... no matter which box you choose a package from.

AQUINAS: If this is a cookie sale, why are we selling them for more than the market in Chadron sells them for?

HOOLEY: (*He stares at her blouse.*) Aquinas, your two top buttons are undone.

AQUINAS: It's close in the store today.

HOOLEY: Button up. We have to appear and act professionally.

AQUINAS: And unattractive.

HOOLEY: Unattractive? What are you shitting on about, Aquinas? Unattractive.

AQUINAS: Hooley, am I more attractive or less attractive with a button or two unbuttoned?

HOOLEY: Where did you come upon such a rancid question?

(O'GARR *enters, Western shirt, clean jeans, boots, going-to-town straw Stetson.*)

HOOLEY: O'Garr, the finest of our ranchers.

O'GARR: (*Hands* HOOLEY *a slip of paper.*) Here's an order. I'm going to jog to the bar… pay my tab.

HOOLEY: You can count on us, O'Garr.

O'GARR: Nice day, Aquinas. (O'GARR *exits.*)

HOOLEY: Acts like nobility, he does. Ascendancy class, ill-mannered chunk-of-shit.

AQUINAS: O'Garr is always pleasant to me.

HOOLEY: How pleasant?

AQUINAS: Pleasant. He smiles, says hello.

HOOLEY: Is O'Garr more or less pleasant when you have yourself immodestly unbuttoned?

AQUINAS: What if a customer tells me the Verona cookies are only $3.25 at the supermarket in Chadron?

HOOLEY: Tell them to buy gas and drive to Chadron! (HOOLEY *suddenly strikes* AQUINAS, *knocks her sideways to the floor.*) See what you made me do? (HOOLEY *helps* AQUINAS *get up, clutches her.*)

AQUINAS: I'm sorry, John.

(O'GARR *enters.*)

O'GARR: Hooley, if you want to run a store, it's all failure if you have a jammed front door. Noon is when people go for what they need. Is my stuff ready or not?

HOOLEY: Just a small delay, O'Garr. Confusion over shelving.

O'GARR: Hooley, bounce! I came by with a list, goddamnit! Bounce!

(HOOLEY *scrambles to please* O'GARR, *knocks over a chair.*)

Scene Nine

(DQ *has tricked herself out in zippy cut-off Levi jeans and a cherry-red scoop neck blouse with a push-up bra beneath it. She has ballet slippers on her feet, sunglasses over her eyes.* MOSS *is looking like himself.*)

MOSS: If you behave yourself, I'll get us ice cream sandwiches.

DQ: Check the expiration dates. (*Waves to someone off stage.*) Hi, fart-knucks!

MOSS: There you go again… making people hate you when they want to love you.

DQ: Maybe love is only temporary. (*Pause.*) My daddy… my daddy hung hisself from a barn rafter.

MOSS: No, he didn't.

DQ: I know. But I like to pretend. It's better 'n them runnin' off 'n leavin' me.

MOSS: You want to go somewheres?

DQ: Naw… I was just contemplating my virginity. (*Pause.*) You ever think about your virginity?

MOSS: What the hell are you talking about, DQ?

DQ: My virginity.

MOSS: I don't want none of this talk.

DQ: You rather contemplate how this town is dyin'?

MOSS: I better get the ice cream sandwiches.

DQ: This town does not contribute to our nation's birth rate. You ever think on that, Moss?

MOSS: Never.

DQ: Ain't been a child born in this town in two years. Girls get pregnant, but they go calve-out in North Platte… or Denver… if they got money. And they don't come back, at least not with a baby.

MOSS: Maybe O'Garr and his new wife will cure that.

DQ: If no one's being born, how long's it gonna be before this is a ghost town? (*Pause.*) Course you and I could take it up.

MOSS: Ain't interested.

DQ: We could be modern day Adam and Eve.

MOSS: You got mental afflictions.

(DQ *performs an Irish jig, turns it into a waltz with an unwilling* MOSS, *then turns her dance grotesque with a few beats of Butoh dance.*)

Scene Ten

(*Night...* O'GARR's *ranch yard lit by 300-watt bulbs here and there, creating shadows.* O'GARR *is on a porch chair, cleaning a revolver. He is in jeans, T-shirt, boots. He is waiting... rubbing his revolver with a rag, impatient. We hear a car approach, wheels on a gravel driveway.* O'GARR, *holding onto the gun, stands, waits. Car doors open and close.* CINTHIA *and* HOOLEY *enter.*
CINTHIA *is wearing an expensive cream-colored low-cut sheath dress with a Western belt... huge belt buckle... and she is carrying a pair of high heel shoes.* HOOLEY *is in work clothes.*)

CINTHIA: You should have been there, sweetheart. The town can really be something special.

HOOLEY: Your wife is an organizational whiz!

O'GARR: I'd invite you in, Hooley, but ranchers rise early.

HOOLEY: Absolutely.

(HOOLEY *starts to exit, but* CINTHIA *grabs him, turns him around.*)

CINTHIA: Hooley get the clipboard. Let's review the progress. My sour-puss husband needs to know things are finally shaking around here.

(HOOLEY *exits*.)

O'GARR: Get rid of that imbecile.

CINTHIA: Patience, sweetheart, patience. (*Touches him affectionately*.) Then I might invite you to take this dress off… with your teeth.

O'GARR: Where the fuck were you?

CINTHIA: I am the new vice president of the brand new Development Council. (*Pause*.) You could participate, help make this town viable.

O'GARR: I come in from workin' and you're gone. No note.

CINTHIA: You'd be in the loop if you'd get a cell phone.

O'GARR: Cell phones are for city people who imagine they're important, when they ain't at all.

(HOOLEY *enters with a clipboard*.)

CINTHIA: Let's begin, Hooley, with the month by month event schedule.

O'GARR: Hooley, you must be eager to get back to Aquinas.

HOOLEY: That's the strange of it. Aquinas has taken to… long walks.   Don't know what to make of it.

CINTHIA: Now, now, Hooley, every future January will feature…?

HOOLEY: (*Puts on glasses, finds a light source from which to read from.*)   January: We shall have a High Plains Art and Photography Competition Show. The old hospital is empty… and there are a dozen rooms fit for exhibiting art.

O'GARR: Who could be against pictures of naked women?

HOOLEY: There'll be none of that. We want to draw into town the largest number of people. People with morals.

CINTHIA: And people with dollars. These will largely be day visitors. But with upgrades to the Roche Motel…

O'GARR: And a goddamned name change.

HOOLEY: (*Looks at his clipboard.*) And in February…

O'GARR: In February I have early calving… and that's a business Cinthia can learn.

CINTHIA: And in March, Sweetheart…

O'GARR: …we'll have epic goddamned blizzards and ragin' winds outta the North fuckin' Pole.

CINTHIA: …and in March we'll have the annual High Plains Film Festival… with some old cowboy actor like John Wayne as co-host.

O'GARR: John Wayne's dead… about as dead as Wyatt fucking Earp is ever gonna be.

HOOLEY: We can hire a John Wayne look-alike.

CINTHIA: April will be for our annual gun show. Sweetheart, you love guns, right?

O'GARR: I don't love guns. I love shooting things. Collectors like guns, because gun collectors ain't got dicks. Me, I just kill things I sometimes eat. (*Pause.*) Cinthia, there ain't enough room in town for any of this. Who'd want to stay in the Roche Motel?

CINTHIA: May will be High Plains Rodeo Month. And June…

O'GARR: (*Points gun at* HOOLEY.) You know the saying, Hooley, right? "All guns are loaded all the time." What we have here is me offering a clinic in poor firearms safety.

HOOLEY: 'Night folks. (HOOLEY *exits*.)

CINTHIA: You sonofabitch!

O'GARR: (*Tries to embrace her.*) It's not loaded.

CINTHIA: You said it was loaded.

O'GARR: No, Cin, I just offered a maxim… a saying.

CINTHIA: You don't offer a damned thing pointing a gun at the head of one of our friends.

O'GARR: Friend? Hooley is no friend of mine. He may be your friend, but that is too weird for me to assimilate.

CINTHIA: Why are you so down on people?

(*After a pause, with her back to the audience, facing* O'GARR, CINTHIA *lowers the top of her dress.*)

Scene Eleven

(Florescent light in a decommissioned missile silo. A gray metal table with charts and maps on it. Half awake, in a man's bathrobe, WAITRESS shambles in on her entrance, looks around. She sits on a fake leather plastic sofa. WAITRESS stands, goes to the table, examines the maps and charts, holds them up, sets them down, time and time again.)

WAITRESS: *(Calls out.)* What're all these maps?

(KEN, *in shorts, leg brace, and an Army T-shirt, enters, carries in pre-packaged morning pastries and two glasses of orange juice.*)

KEN: The most important meal of the day, breakfast. But this is what's in the cupboard.

WAITRESS: *(Casts a hard look at the pastries.)* How old?

KEN: Good for another twenty years.

(They begin to eat.)

WAITRESS: What're the maps for?

KEN: I should call you Cinderella.
WAITRESS: Cinderella gets killed in the end.

KEN: What? No. Cinderella marries the prince.

WAITRESS: Some prince. I don't even know who the hell you are. (*Pause.*) These pastries are dry. We shoulda driven to the café. I coulda cooked a breakfast.

KEN: Now that you know where I live, I'll stock fresher pastries.

WAITRESS: Your maps… they're all local.

KEN: My new hobby.

WAITRESS: Maps are your hobby.

KEN: Water's my new hobby.

WAITRESS: Nobody's got a water hobby. Stop bullshitting.

KEN: Water is the liquid of the 21st century. It's in a book called *The Coming Anarchy*. Yep… water, sweet deep-aquifer water… liquid of the 21st century.

WAITRESS: That's diarrhea on a fruitcake, Ken. Oil is the liquid of this and all future centuries.

KEN: Oil is 20th century. Water is our Desperate-Now. Water and war are going to walk hand in hand pretty darned soon.

WAITRESS: You have drifted to the wrong fucking place, Mr. Adams.

KEN: Oh, Cinderella. Yours is a kingdom of clean, sweet, precious water.

WAITRESS: I am not Cinderella.

KEN: The maps… they're a guide to water. Underground water. To an ocean of fresh, sweet, drinkable water. That's my hobby. I am a fan of water… a huge fan of water.

WAITRESS: (*Pause.*) Because you see money in it somehow. Which is wrong. No one should own sunlight and no one should own water.

KEN: Who owns the café?

WAITRESS: I do.

KEN: The Indians that were here not too long ago, they didn't believe that any man could own land. It was an alien concept. (*Pause.*) Let's take a shower.

WAITRESS: I can do that in town.

KEN: A shower could be a lot more fun here.

WAITRESS: If a person lifts weights… or runs every day…

KEN: Yes?

WAITRESS: It's preparation for some sport, right?

KEN: Maybe. Or it's someone who just cares about being healthy.

WAITRESS: And a man who collects maps of the High Plains and underground water?

KEN: No mystery. We've known about and used this underground water for decades and decades. It's the Ogallala Aquifer… sometimes called the "High Plains Aquifer." As far south as Texas, farmers have drilled it for irrigation. A few years ago, a Texas oilman, T. Boone Pickens, started buying up water rights all across the Texas Panhandle.

WAITRESS: I hear a swindle… a raw deal.

KEN: Nothing raw… unless nature and progress are raw deals. Look at the Sandhills just a few miles east of here. Those center pivot farm operations depend almost entirely on the Ogallala Aquifer.

(KEN *places a chunk of pastry between her lips, nibbles toward a kiss… and his free hand reconnoiters the territory warm within her bathrobe.*)

Scene Twelve

(*A mile or two beyond the town limits,* DQ *and* MOSS *are sitting on a short stack of bales of alfalfa or hay.* MOSS *is in jeans, a raggedy Western shirt, and boots.* DQ *is similarly dressed: jeans, a tied-at-the-ribs cowgirl shirt, running shoes.*)

MOSS: I don't have the grades to be an astronaut, but pretty soon all kinds of people are going up to space… to colonies on Mars. (*Pause.*) That ain't such a bad dream.

DQ: Guess it's what picture frame you put around a dream.

MOSS: Someday there'll be mining operations on Mars… sending back rare minerals.

DQ: So that's why there's stuff you walk away from… because you have this dream.

MOSS: What-all do I walk away from?

DQ: You never get into knuckle-ups with other guys.

MOSS: I'd get my sorry ass kicked in a fight.

DQ: Not if the fight was worth carin' about.
MOSS: You got it all figured out.

DQ: Not really.

MOSS: And you keep landin' on your feet.

DQ: A room at the Roche Motel… being a ward of this town: that doesn't sound like I land well at all.

MOSS: But it's freedom. You don't answer to anybody.

DQ: You're pretty free yourself, Moss.

MOSS: (*Pause.*) You ever wonder how it's gonna turn out… like in two years when school is done for?

DQ: It'd be nice to walk into church with a dollar for the collection plate. (Pause.) Waking up in a five-star Sun Valley resort hotel would be nice. A wedge of cheese, hot coffee, pulpy orange juice for breakfast. Free plush bathrobe you can take home with you, 'cause the rich never wear the same clothes twice. (*Pause.*) Like… I was reading one time, Bill Clinton donates all his underpants to charity.

MOSS: You're making this up, DQ. Just when we get to havin' a serious talk, you run off some bullshit about Bill Clinton's underpants.

DQ: It's true, Moss, swear-to-God true. Bill Clinton donates his underpants, just worn once, to charity.

MOSS: You're crazy.

DQ: It's a tax deal. Bill Clinton writes off his underwear. It's a tax deduction.

MOSS: You can't get a tax deduction from underwear.

DQ: Sure you can. You stockpile your dirty underwear until there's a washer load. You wash your underpants. You stack them in piles of a dozen each. You shrink-wrap 'em. You drive your saved-up, used underpants to Goodwill in Lincoln. They give you a receipt for the value of your donation. That, Moss, is called documentation. (*Pause.* DQ *laughs.*) That was too fuckin' easy.

MOSS: Guess that's why we're best friends, DQ. You always amaze me.

DQ: (*Pause.*) Who do you picture in your head when you go to fiddlin'.

MOSS: I don't fiddle.

DQ: Waitress says all guys are self-fiddlers.

MOSS: Not me.

DQ: Waitress says men lie about self-fiddlin'. Women fall into two groups.

MOSS: You need to stop this line of talk.

DQ: There's women who fiddle themselves. And they's dried-out ones ain't never been moist.

MOSS: Waitress is a pervert.

DQ: No, she ain't. Waitress gives you and me a lot of free sandwiches, free soda pop, free ice cream… and sometimes she slips me a ten dollar bill. (*Pause.*) You gonna answer?

MOSS: Answer?

DQ: Do I come to you like a vision when you're fiddlin'? Yes or fucking no?

MOSS: I'm leavin'.

(MOSS *and* DQ sit quietly for a moment. MOSS *moves away from* DQ.)

DQ: Moss, you like my eyes? (*No response from him.*) Eyes get mentioned a lot in songs.

MOSS: Didn't know you gave any of that crap any thought.

DQ: Like… you ever picture me in a bedroom with scented candles all lit and glowin'?

MOSS: Can't say that I have.

DQ: Give me your hand.

MOSS: No thanks.

DQ: No tricks or jokes. Just give me your hand.

MOSS: You can't be trusted.

DQ: Trust me this once. See, by holdin' your hand, I can tell if you're a liar. (*Pause.*) It's about measuring the hand's heat, which is about blood flow. If a guy lies, his hands give him away.

(MOSS *gives his hand to* DQ. *She places it against her chest... and he yanks it free.*)

DQ: You feel my heart? It's faster this afternoon.

(DQ *again places his hand on her breast, pulls his snap shirt open... leans forward, kisses his chest. They start to make-out. She leads him behind the bales. Shirts are tossed onto the bales from the hidden side. After a few beats,* AQUINAS *enters quietly, aware, and listens.* AQUINAS *is wearing a rolled-up-at-the-waist skirt and her off-white blouse is unbuttoned to a bra covered by a slip top.* AQUINAS *sits on a bale, folds her arms across her chest, listens to* MOSS *and* DQ *as they begin to make love. As* MOSS *and* DQ *get louder, a smiling*

AQUINAS *crawls away, placing a hand over her mouth… as if to stifle laughter of discovery, delight, and joy.*)

Scene Thirteen

(*Sunset: the bales. Alone,* AQUINAS *appears asleep atop the bales, her long hair undone. From a distance come the voices of* FATHER BEN *and* HOOLEY. *They are calling out for* AQUINAS. *Their calls grow near. A pause.* AQUINAS *does not stir.*)

FATHER BEN: (*Off stage, calling out.*) There she is!

HOOLEY: (*Off stage.*) Where? Where is she?

FATHER BEN: (*Off stage.*) To your east. At the bales!

(AQUINAS *stretches, slowly sits up as* FATHER BEN *enters.*)

FATHER BEN: Aquinas, are you okay?

AQUINAS: I had a vision.

(HOOLEY *enters, dressed in his customary store owner's outfit.*)

HOOLEY: This time you've done it, Aquinas, really been the slack-jaw bitch.

FATHER BEN: Are you hungry? We have water in the car.

AQUINAS: It was a beautiful vision.

HOOLEY: Her head's full of horse hair.

AQUINAS: I saw… saw how beautiful and simple it can be.

HOOLEY: Simple! For twenty dollars up front, I'd sell you to Arabs!

FATHER BEN: Aquinas, what happened? (*Points to her unbuttoned blouse.*) Did someone harm you?

HOOLEY: Harm? I should beat her until she yelps and moans like the dumb alley bitch that she is.

FATHER BEN: Preserve yourself, Hooley.

HOOLEY: I had to close up early, Aquinas. Early! That's lost money.

FATHER BEN: She needs water.

HOOLEY: You look like a common railroad whore. Button up! Do I have to put you in some asylum?

FATHER BEN: Aquinas needs water.

HOOLEY: No. We'll take her back. Let her drink from the hose behind the store.

AQUINAS: Father, do you believe...?

HOOLEY: Aquinas, what has curdled your mind?

AQUINAS: ... do you think that we can have a portion of heaven right here?

(HOOLEY *grips* AQUINAS' *arm, starts to lead her... but she breaks free.*)

AQUINAS: I don't think I want to...

HOOLEY: Come on! (HOOLEY *grabs her again.*) I've come for you. Come with me!

FATHER BEN: Gentle, Hooley, gentle. We don't know what's happened.

AQUINAS: I don't want to go back.

HOOLEY: You don't want to go back?

AQUINAS: The store is not my place. It's a grave.

HOOLEY: I'm losing patience, Aquinas.

AQUINAS: Is it a sin, Father Ben, if a girl gives a boy a jar of white mulberry preserves?

HOOLEY: She's a lunatic.

FATHER BEN: What about mulberry preserves?

AQUINAS: If a girl brings a boy a jar of mulberry preserves…

FATHER BEN: Yes?

AQUINAS: A gift.

FATHER BEN: There's no sin in giving gifts, Aquinas. Did you give a jar of jam or preserves from Hooley's store?

HOOLEY: No surprise if she did. I've been too lax with the inventory.

AQUINAS: Father, the purpose was something different.

HOOLEY: Get to the car, Aquinas, or this will get harsh.

AQUINAS: Is it a sin, Father Ben, if the girl invites the boy to spread preserves across her skin?

HOOLEY: That's it!

(HOOLEY *grabs* AQUINAS. *She resists and he clobbers her.* AQUINAS *goes to the ground, knocked out.*)

FATHER BEN: What have you done? (*He kneels, checks her pulse.*) You've killed her.

HOOLEY: Impossible. No such good luck. (*He kneels, touches her wrist and then her neck.*) You fool, Ben, she's just asleep.

FATHER BEN: She's not sleeping, Hooley. She's dead.

HOOLEY: When I piss on her, she'll come to right quick. (*Picks up* AQUINAS *from under her arms.*) Take her by the ankles.

FATHER BEN: Leave her be. I'll get some water.

(HOOLEY *lets her down.* AQUINAS *moans.* FATHER BEN *exits.*)

HOOLEY: After all I've done, this is the way kindness is repaid. (*Gives her a kick in the ribs.*) There's going to be a new regime, Aquinas. I'll chain you like a mutt bitch. Chain you, chain, chain, chain you! (*Pause. A thought.*) Have you been meeting a lover? That's it, right, Aquinas? You come out here and some man rubs you down with fruit preserves stolen from my store?

(FATHER BEN *enters with a 20-ounce bottle of water.*)

HOOLEY: Who do you thinks she's been screwing, Ben, screwing behind my back?

FATHER BEN (*Pours a trickle of water on her brow.*) Hooley, catch yourself.

HOOLEY: She's been giving my name a black mark, Ben. That's why she's out here. (*Looks around.*) Ben, her lover ran off when we drove up. That's what happened.

(FATHER BEN *strokes* AQUINAS' *hair. She stirs.*)

HOOLEY: (*Gives her a small kick.*) Get up, Aquinas.

AQUINAS: (*Hesitantly.*) I'm not going back.

HOOLEY: You need more discipline? I'm the man for the job.

FATHER BEN: Get away from her, Hooley.

HOOLEY: "Get away from her, Hooley"? Are those the words that just came from your mouth, Ben? (*Pause. He turns his back.*) You can both walk back to town. (HOOLEY *exits.*)

Scene Fourteen

(*Office of the Roche Motel. In jeans and T-shirt,* MOSS *is on his belly on the floor, handcuffed.* ISABELLE *is nearby, smoking a cigarette, dressed to handle tasks at check-out time.* LOUIE *enters, drying his hands with a large bath towel. He's rumpled.*)

LOUIE: (*Snaps the towel at* MOSS.) Defrauding an inn keeper is a federal offense, you little shit.

MOSS: I can work it off.

LOUIE: Plus you coulda set the motel on fire... flickering candles! Goin' to sleep with candles lit. You have any idea how many motels burn to the ground 'cause of candles? Hundreds every year.

ISABELLE: Louie.

LOUIE: What, Isabelle, what?

ISABELLE: You were going to canvas town again for the development project.

LOUIE: Well, this little shit and DQ... well this fucker is not going to cheat me out of a night's rent.

ISABELLE: Is she okay?

LOUIE: DQ's cuffed to the bathroom sink.

MOSS: You better not have hurt her.

LOUIE: (*Snaps the towel at* MOSS *again.*) One of you owes me $35. You tried to elude me. That means you were running out on motel rent. You thought you could cheat ol' Louie, did ya? You sure was surprised. Tackled you right in the parking lot. Just like in Division I on-fucking-TV football. Tackled the righteous fuck out of you. You think $35 is nothing? You think I'd let $35 slip by as this town struggles to survive…

ISABELLE: Louie.

LOUIE: Jesus, Isabelle, what?

ISABELLE: Give me the key to the cuffs.

LOUIE: No!

ISABELLE: We can't keep DQ chained up.

LOUIE: DQ ain't chained, Isabelle. She is cuffed. Comfortably cuffed if she doesn't resist.

ISABELLE: Is she half naked, Louie?

MOSS: That's false imprisonment, Louie… and that is a federal crime.

ISABELLE: Louie, the key! Someone comes by, they'll think it's a sex crime.

MOSS: Yeah, Louie Roche, someone's gonna think you're a deviant.

(LOUIE *drops down, whacks* MOSS, *begins to choke him.* ISABELLE *pulls* LOUIE *off.*)

ISABELLE: This is over $35, Louie, $35 above the $450 a month the town pays us to lodge DQ?

LOUIE: First principle: Moss owes us $35 because he stayed the night.

ISABELLE: Louie, a single night is $35… and one additional person is $10. So Moss owes us ten, Louie, not thirty-five.

LOUIE: Isabelle, are you switching sides?

(DQ *enters, mostly snapped-up Western shirt on, not much else… no cuffs. She's got a piece of sink pipe in her hand.*)

DQ: Set Moss loose!

ISABELLE: (*Softly, to* DQ.) Hi, honey.

LOUIE: How'd you break free? You wreck my plumbing? You gotta pay damages!

(O'GARR *enters in going-to-town Western clothes. He takes in the scene, removes a can of Copenhagen Snuff from a shirt pocket, puts a good-size pinch beneath his lower lip.*)

O'GARR: Another reenactment, Louie?

LOUIE: These little criminals tried to cheat me.

MOSS: O'Garr, tell him to cut me loose.

O'GARR: What'd they do, keep company all night in DQ's room?

LOUIE: That's what they did. And Moss owes me $35.

ISABELLE: Or ten… depending on your logic.

LOUIE: It's thirty-goddamned-five dollars… that's what this motel is owed.

O'GARR: I'm surprised it's taken 'em this long. (O'GARR *takes out a roll of bills, sets down some money.*) Must be thirty or so dollars there, Louie. You can count it later.

LOUIE: You don't have to do this, O'Garr.

O'GARR: Don't I know it.

(LOUIE *snatches up the money, finds a handcuffs key, hands it to* ISABELLE… *and she frees* MOSS. *Arms around each other,* DQ *and* MOSS *exit*.)

LOUIE: I appreciate that, O'Garr. That is real cowboy of you!

ISABELLE: And real mercantile of you, Louie. Screw it, I need to find a couple shots of whiskey. (ISABELLE *exits*.)

LOUIE: You're a true man of the West, O'Garr. The two of us, the two of us together, we can save this town. We can develop it.

O'GARR: Let's keep 'er short this morning. (*Pause.*) First off, Moss will be keeping company with DQ… in her room… not a cent charged to either of 'em. Got that?

LOUIE: That doesn't take into account…

O'GARR: Not a cent charged! Got that?
(LOUIE *nods*.)

O'GARR: They're just talkin' all night, far as you're concerned. Ain't none of your business. A portion of happiness needs to be free, right, Louie?

LOUIE: I guess.

O'GARR: Second, did my wife give you a check for a thousand dollars?

LOUIE: You mean yesterday?

O'GARR: Louie, does Cinthia give you a check every fucking day?

LOUIE: Then we're talking yesterday.

O'GARR: What for?

LOUIE: The money?

O'GARR: Are you trying to take a bite of me?

LOUIE: A bite of you?

O'GARR: My money is <u>me</u>. My cows are <u>me</u>. Cinthia is a part of <u>me</u>. (*Pause.*) Jesus syphilitic Christ, wipe off your mouth, Louie.

LOUIE: Wipe off my mouth?

O'GARR: Your lips are wet… like you been suckin' on somebody.

LOUIE: (*Wipes his mouth with his jacket sleeve.*) Cinthia and me… we just happened to talk… on this 'n that.

O'GARR: So she writes you a check for a grand? Over talk?

LOUIE: See… she was askin' after DQ.

O'GARR: Yep.

LOUIE: And Cinthia reckons that DQ needs clothes. Thinks DQ appears raggedly. And Cinthia… she says to me, "I want to give you some money to properly dress DQ." Cinthia asks if Isabelle can take DQ down to Ogalala for some clothes…

O'GARR: No sixteen-year-old girl needs a thousand dollars for clothes… not at one gulp.

LOUIE: You wouldn't think so. But I didn't want no argument. (Pause.) Well… the money wasn't all to be for clothes.

O'GARR: Yep.

LOUIE: Cinthia says to me… she says, "Whatever's left over from the shoppin', well, you take it as a donation to the development committee.

O'GARR: You got the check still?

LOUIE: It's right here. (*He motions.*)

O'GARR: Give it to me.

LOUIE: What'll I say to your wife?

O'GARR: Whatever the fuck you usually say.

(LOUIE *finds the check, hands it to* O'GARR, *who takes out a roll of bills and peels off a few.*)

O'GARR: Here's $500 in folding money.

(LOUIE *accepts the cash as* O'GARR *rips up the check and lets the paper flutter to the floor.*)

LOUIE: How is the money to be divided?

O'GARR: It's all for DQ… for clothes.

LOUIE: What about saving this town, what about development… seed money?

(*Laughing,* O'GARR *gets* LOUIE *in a headlock and gives him a noogie.*)

O'GARR: Next time I won't be amused to just give you a noogie.

Scene Fifteen

(*Interior of Hooley's store.* HOOLEY, *head down, sits on a checkout counter. He picks up a duster and whacks the counter a few times.* FATHER BEN *enters.*)

HOOLEY: You're as useful as an empty bottle of cheapjack tequila. You're like a pesky bladder infection. Like wind-drift newspapers out on Main Street.

FATHER BEN: These are hard days, Hooley.

HOOLEY: Nice of you to say that. Don't be fizzy and fuzzy. Spill whatever you know. With Aquinas leaving, it sure as hell ain't too soon for everything I'll ever know. (*Pause.*) I'd like to hear Aquinas scream just once more in pain. (*Pause.*) The store is in dismal shape.

(CINTHIA *enters in a sprightly top and tight jeans and fashion sunglasses, leading* AQUINAS, *who is dressed in a skirt and white blouse.* AQUINAS *is carrying a stuffed and bulging, small lightweight travel bag.* FATHER BEN *and* CINTHIA *position themselves so as to be bodyguards for* AQUINAS.)

HOOLEY: I have a few dollars for you, Aquinas.

(HOOLEY *takes a few bills from his pocket and tries to walk the money to* AQUINAS, *but is blocked off.*)

AQUINAS: I don't want money.

CINTHIA: (*To* AQUINAS.) Yes, you do want money.

AQUINAS: It's filthy. The money. Ugly money.

(CINTHIA *takes the money from* HOOLEY. AQUINAS *exits, followed by* CINTHIA. FATHER BEN *plays the rear guard, but….*)

HOOLEY: Wait, Ben.

FATHER BEN: There'll be a court order to keep you away from my church, home, and the church grounds… until Aquinas leaves town. Then our friendship, if you care to retain it, may continue.

HOOLEY: Aquinas getting a lawyer?

FATHER BEN: Mrs. O'Garr is seeing to it.

HOOLEY: They'll leave me with nothing.

FATHER BEN: (*Looks around.*) This is everything?

HOOLEY: It's what I've got.

(KEN *enters, nods to* FATHER BEN, *who exits.*)

KEN: Friend, I know the mood that you're in.

HOOLEY: You know my mood.

KEN: I am here to talk about hope. Reclaiming hope.

HOOLEY: Not interested.

KEN: I have known trauma, Hooley, so I know how to help you. (*Pause.*) Friends do not abandon friends in hard times.

HOOLEY: We hardly know one another. And now you're here on my worst day… being my friend?

KEN: That's the way of it.

HOOLEY: To what purpose?

KEN: To help your sorry ass. (*Pause.*) Hooley, I <u>like</u> this town. I own property <u>here</u>. The ongoing <u>success</u> of your store is in my interest. Do I want to do all my shopping in Chadron or south in North Platte? Hell no! It's real nice to know you're here… with just the right item to get a man or family through a night. Out of light bulbs? Hooley has 'em. Need spaghetti? Hooley has boxes of pasta.

HOOLEY: Aquinas will have a lawyer on my back before long. I won't be able to hold out.

KEN: Let me help.

HOOLEY: You got loose change? I'm payments behind to distributors. Aquinas will get half the value of this place. You a rich man?

KEN: It'll take far less up-front cash than you think.

(WAITRESS *enters in a gingham outfit that displays her breasts and legs to advantage. She is carrying a six-pack of beer, a laptop, and a briefcase.*)

WAITRESS: The party goin' yet or you boys awaitin' for me?

KEN: Hooley, a new chapter of your life is beginning.

WAITRESS: (*Hands a beer to each man.*) Cool beer… perfect for a hot-ass day on the plains.

KEN: Hooley, allow me to surprise you.

HOOLEY: I've had enough surprises.

(KEN *goes to the briefcase, opens it, takes out a stack of cash, hands it to* HOOLEY.)

HOOLEY: What's this?

KEN: A small loan. One-percent interest. There's five grand there, Hooley… and that will pay off your distributors. You can order fresh product now.

HOOLEY: I don't want a loan.

KEN: Sure you do.

HOOLEY: I can't pay you back, not from this store. Five-thousand dollars? I couldn't pay that back in five years.

KEN: That's where you're wrong, Hooley. Tonight we have a small party. We talk it all over tomorrow. Now's the time to erase pain.

(WAITRESS *opens up the laptop as the men suck on their beers, turns it so that* HOOLEY *can see what she's found.*)

WAITRESS: These'll make you forget Aquinas real quick.

HOOLEY: What the hell is this?

KEN: Waitress has a solution for your companionship problem.

HOOLEY: (*Looks at the computer screen.*) Russiangirls.com? (*Pause.*) Even if I wanted a Russian girl, I don't even have the cash for gas all the way to Omaha and back.

KEN: Relax, Hooley. These ladies come right to you. (*Pause.*) Where'd you find Aquinas?

HOOLEY: A convent. She was an orphan of some nature. (*Pause.*) A Russian woman?

KEN: One of their girls can be here in forty-eight hours.

HOOLEY: I've done some things, Ken, but I don't want any part of whatever this is.

WAITRESS: I was suspicious of Ken, too. But trust him.

HOOLEY: Who's paying for all of this?

KEN: Just a credit card no one cares a whole lot about.

HOOLEY: Whose credit card is it?

KEN: (*Pause.*) Rich guys. Water guys. I do favors for them. A few thousand dollars is nothing for the water industry guys… nothing at all. Want to lease a Russian girl, so what? We're gonna find you a sweet one. She might love it out here. All you have to do is pick her from the computer. Before long, she'll make you forget Aquinas.

HOOLEY: What kind of documents am I gonna have to sign?

KEN: This is the West, isn't it? Let's just shake hands and partner-up.

(WAITRESS *gently pushes* HOOLEY *toward* KEN. KEN *shakes* HOOLEY's *hand.*)

Scene Sixteen

(FATHER BEN *and* AQUINAS *are reading. He has a Bible open.* AQUINAS *is thumbing through a stack of* People *magazines.* FATHER BEN *is in black trousers, a white* dress shirt, *slippers.* AQUINAS *is in a new sundress and sandals. They are at a remove, each in a comfortable chair.*).

FATHER BEN: This book always turns out the same. Without variation. But the interpretation riddles us. In the early days of the church, they debated what kind of appearance Jesus had.

AQUINAS: That's sinful.

FATHER BEN: (*Considers the notion.*) More political than sinful. By the time of the controversy, Jesus was long-crucified. (*Pause.*) There were two schools of thought. One group thought that Jesus was average to ugly… since most of us are concocted to that appearance.

AQUINAS: Jesus was not ugly!

FATHER BEN: Your outlook, the views of the 2nd group, won out. It was decided that Jesus was, indeed, handsome.

AQUINAS: He was.

FATHER BEN: But then the question arose: how handsome was Jesus. Was He virile in appearance… or was he prettier than handsome?

AQUINAS: Those questions should never have been asked.

FATHER BEN: When you were a girl in the convent, what appearance did Jesus have? Was he fair-skinned and blonde… or was he Jewish in appearance?

AQUINAS: I'm not telling.

FATHER BEN: What? (*Pause.*) Aquinas… was Jesus blonde or was he dark-haired? Was he portrayed in convent art as tall and slender, tall and muscular, or was he dark-skinned, short-of-stature, filthy-haired, with a soiled robe?

AQUINAS: Father, are you baiting me?

FATHER BEN: How can we worship what we cannot envision? Do you picture Jesus in your mind when you pray?

AQUINAS: And what does Jesus look like in your brain?

FATHER BEN: Like some Israeli rock 'n roll singer.

AQUINAS: Blasphemy!

FATHER BEN: (*Gently laughs.*) You certainly are good company, Aquinas. You have brightened these past couple of days. (*Pause as she looks down.*) How's the *People* magazine project going?

AQUINAS: Cinthia has me on the wrong track. I'm a daydreamer… and sometimes a toiler. I like to work… keep busy. This magazine is mere gossip.

FATHER BEN: She has her ideas, doesn't she?

AQUINAS: First *People*. Then *Time*. Then a week of TV nights at the O'Garr's. Then fashion magazines. But where can it all end?

FATHER BEN: Isn't that now your choice?

AQUINAS: What if I want to walk? What if I want to walk whichever way the wind blows? One day walk south. One day walk southeast, then turn north with a change of wind. That'd be something, wouldn't it?

FATHER BEN: What about food?

AQUINAS: I could eat about anything. Whatever I found. And I don't eat much. Hooley made me nervous about eating. "That's our profit," he'd say, then point at my plate.

FATHER BEN: You're through with Hooley. He knows better than to look for you.

AQUINAS: You don't know John Hooley.

FATHER BEN: I do know Hooley. He calculates what he can get away with… and he knows when he's out of his depth.

AQUINAS: I do feel safe here, but….

FATHER BEN: You are safe in this rectory.

AQUINAS: (*Pause.*) Do you think some people are talking? (*Pause.*) You… apparently have a weakness.

FATHER BEN: No one is taking Hooley seriously.

AQUINAS: Me and you… here alone together?

FATHER BEN: Everyone knows this is your temporary shelter. And I am coping with my… attractions… empathy with the opposite gender.

(AQUINAS *exits.* FATHER BEN *reflects. After a moment or two,* AQUINAS *returns with two plates… a slice of cherry pie on each plate. She hands one to* FATHER BEN, *sits down with her pie, watches him start to eat. Flabbergasting* FATHER BEN, AQUINAS *slips out of her sundress, approaches him, takes pie from the plate and offers it to his mouth.* FATHER BEN *leans back to avoid her.* AQUINAS *sits on his lap, takes a bite of pie, begins kissing him. At first stolid,* FATHER BEN *participates in her passion. The moment is soon shattered by the sound of a door being kicked-in.* HOOLEY *enters with a baseball bat… takes the scene into his booze-flooded brain.)*

HOOLEY: My wife with you? With you, Ben?

(*As* HOOLEY *approaches,* FATHER BEN *and* AQUINAS *separate.*)

FATHER BEN: Get out of here, Hooley! I'm calling the sheriff.

(AQUINAS *cowers in a corner, moans as if expecting a beating.*)

HOOLEY: Aquinas, make yourself modest!

(AQUINAS *shudders, draws further into herself, into this nightmare, and she keens.*)

HOOLEY: I won't be patient for long, Aquinas.

FATHER BEN: (*Edges off, as if to reach a land line telephone.*) Hooley, you'd best leave.

HOOLEY: (*Waving and swinging the bat for punctuation.*) My former friend and my wife! Fucking. You want Aquinas?

You want this hellish brain clot in a woman's body? You want her sweat-stained floral-blue bra and her piss-stink panties in your hands and mouth? <u>Aquinas… is…my… scorched oatmeal… wormy bacon… powdered eggs!</u> That's our fate. She can't help it. She likes the bargain. And I won't give her up… not to you.

FATHER BEN: Please, Hooley, please.

AQUINAS: (*Softly.*) I'll come, John.

HOOLEY: You'll come on your hands and knees… crawl up to the store in your bra and panties… crawl like the crazy whore you've become.

(*As* AQUINAS *begins a moaning crawl,* CINTHIA *enters… holding a pistol.*)

CINTHIA: Enough! Hooley! Enough!

(HOOLEY *lurches at* CINTHIA, *the bat cocked for a swing.* CINTHIA *gut-shoots* HOOLEY. AQUINAS *scrambles to* FATHER BEN, *who protectively embraces her.* AQUINAS *holds on to* FATHER BEN. HOOLEY, *in agony, yelps.* CINTHIA *approaches* HOOLEY, *shoots him in the side of his head.*)

Scene Seventeen

(*Florescent light in* KEN's *missile silo. A gray metal table with charts and maps on it.* MOSS *and* DQ *are trading paperwork, hand it back and forth. In his free hand,* MOSS *has a strong flashlight. He is in jeans and T-shirt, running shoes.* DQ *has a windbreaker on over a T-shirt and jeans, and has on running shoes.* MOSS, *cold and edgy and trying hard to conceal both conditions, flips on the flashlight... and exits.*)

DQ: Don't go far. The place likely has booby traps.

MOSS: (*Off stage.*) Your boobies are traps.

DQ: (*Holds up a county map.*) Ken knows where every well is. He's got 'em marked. Then there's these codes. (*Looks for him.*) Hey, where'd you go?

MOSS: (*Enters, gives in to the cold, hugs himself.*) We better git.

DQ: Goddamn it, I told you to bring a jacket. You're cold. (*Pause.*) It's like he's graded, scored every well in the county. And there's the water sample bottles he's been mailing.

MOSS: Nobody likes pesticides/herbicides in their water. Maybe he's worried for himself. Over east, like in Wayne

County, they got cancer clusters. It's from spraying. Maybe Ken's some sort of green-head.

DQ: This isn't about that. We need to steal this water shit.

MOSS: We're gonna get caught.

DQ: We can prove he's not Mr. Wonderful.

MOSS: I'm for getting out before he elevators down and slits our throats.

DQ: He ain't doing any such.

MOSS: And there we'll be… in a hole. And nobody knowin'. And everybody reckoning we run off to Denver.

DQ: (*Folding some documents.*) Only stupid people run off to Denver.

MOSS: I got a bad feelin'.

DQ: That's 'cause it's ninety-six outside and sixty-nine down here.

MOSS: We shoulda brought a .50 caliber pistol. A .38 won't stop a guy like Ken. He gets wounded… and just keeps comin' at you. He's a Special Forces throat-slittin' maniac with a fake smile.

(WAITRESS *enters.* WAITRESS *is in a new summer dress and sandals… and is putting on a light button-up sweater when she realizes* DQ *and* MOSS *are present. Silence for a few beats.*)

WAITRESS: (*Calling off-stage… nearly singing.*) Sugar…

KEN: (*Off stage.*) Hold on a second.

WAITRESS: I have a surprise for you.

KEN: (*Off stage.*) Outstanding!

WAITRESS: A double surprise.

KEN: (*Off stage.*) I'm up for it. We tried whipped cream on 'em. What've you got in mind?

DQ: Waitress, get us out of this.

WAITRESS: Ken, this is not that kind of surprise.

(KEN *enters. He is wearing khaki shorts, a polo shirt, and cross-trainer shoes.*)

KEN: Everyone empty your pockets.

(MOSS *quickly empties his pockets.* DQ *petulantly tossed folded documents back on the table.*)

WAITRESS: DQ, you're always messin' 'round, but this time…

KEN: Let me take care of this, Waitress. (*To* MOSS *and* DQ.) Been here a while?

(MOSS *and* DQ *shake their heads.* MOSS *looks away.* DQ *holds eye contact with* KEN.)

WAITRESS: Ken, they're just stupid kids.

DQ: Not so stupid as to open my legs for him.

MOSS: DQ, don't piss him off worse.

WAITRESS: Nothin' wrong with Ken. He's real sweet. Generous to boot.

KEN: Waitress, bring us a couple of those kitchen chairs, would ya?

WAITRESS: Do I look like I'm on fuckin' duty, Ken?

KEN: Please, get the chairs, please.

(WAITRESS *exits.*)

KEN: What would you kids do if someone broke into your place?

MOSS: Guess I'd call the sheriff. But that kinda thing just doesn't happen around here.

DQ: (*Over the top of* MOSS.) I'd beat the fuck outta him with whatever's handy.

KEN: (*To* DQ.) I'd wager that you would.

DQ: And if it was some ol' slick like you, I'd finish you off. Take an ice pick to your eyeballs. Then I'd get Moss to help me drag you out to somebody's pick-up. I'd drive your shit-stench carcass outta fuckin' town. I'd dig a hole. Somethin' to fit you. Then I'd pour acid over the top of you… somethin' to make quicker work than dung beetles.

MOSS: Naw, Ken, she wouldn't do any a that at all.

DQ: That's what I would do.

KEN: You ever, DQ, consider serving our country?

DQ: That what you're doin' on the High Plains? Servin' our country? Or are you just out for yourself?

(WAITRESS *enters, dragging on a couple of chairs.* KEN *points to a spot and* WAITRESS *positions the chairs.*)

KEN: Take a load off, kids.

MOSS: Thanks.

DQ: (*Over the top of* MOSS.) You can't make me.

KEN: Sit!

(MOSS *and* DQ *sit. From time to time,* WAITRESS *exits, returns, like a hostess, with store bought cookies and chocolate milk in tall glasses.*)

MOSS: We're expected back to the Roche pretty soon.

KEN: Must have been a nice motor hotel, that's what they were once called, back sixty years ago… before the age of freeways. Now the Roche Motel just needs to be closed. Either a bulldozing or work to make it appear charming in an old-times way.

DQ: I'm outta here. (*She stays seated.*)

KEN: I, personally, not the water corporation that supports my hobby… I, now, own 49% of the Roche Motel. What do you think of that, good investment or bad?

WAITRESS: And I sold Ken 49% of the café, too. For thirty-five grand. And Ken is gonna fix it up so that it looks nineteen-fifties.

KEN: And once Aquinas Hooley gains pause, she'll learn that I bought nearly half of her late husband's store.

DQ: What did anybody here do to deserve gettin' you?

KEN: That's what the Indians around here must have asked… around a hundred and thirty years ago. One Indian says to the other, "Buffalo Hump, what'd we do to deserve these creepy-Christer fat-eating bastards?" (*Pause.*) Human migration. Just keeps happening. Ever since we rose off our knuckles in Africa and headed north to become what we are. (*Pause.*) But it's different now. Thanks to water. Or thanks to the lack of drinking water that's on the horizon.

WAITRESS: Until me 'n Ken got to gettin', I never gave much thought to <u>leaning forward</u>.

KEN: Those who lean forward… they survive. Not just the fittest survive. If you read Darwin, you learn that the adaptable also survive.

DQ: I ain't ever adapting to your bullshit.

KEN: You will, young lady, you will. (*Pause.*) You got the guts of a strong-arm criminal. That will get you through.

(DQ *leaps from her chair, makes a run for it.* KEN *grabs her, loses his grip, goes off balance, and falls.* MOSS *and* DQ *begin to run, but they are thwarted by* WAITRESS, *who smacks* MOSS *with a cookie platter, then seizes* DQ *when she turns back for* MOSS. WAITRESS *and* DQ *wrestle... and finally* KEN *recovers and separates them.* MOSS *sits stunned.*)

DQ: If I get loose, you're going to jail... if I don't kill you first.

KEN: (*Pause.*) No matter what, kid, I get to win. But I like you. Some of the reasons I understand, but others I don't. (KEN *reaches under the table, pulls out an envelope that was taped to its underside.*) You can work for me. (KEN *takes money from the envelope, counts out some of it, gives her cash... and hands* MOSS *cash.*) There's a hundred for each of you. Sure beats the pain in the ass it'd be to take you to the sheriff, to sit through a trial. Let's call it even.

DQ: You can't buy me 'n Moss off.

(DQ *rips the cash up.* MOSS *watches, sticks his money into a pocket.*)

WAITRESS: That's the most idiotic thing you've ever done, DQ.

KEN: That's okay. In two weeks, when the construction crew arrives to remodel the Roche Motel, DQ, you'll be moving to Chadron.

DQ: You can't evict me from the motel.

KEN: You're not being evicted. You're being <u>lodged elsewhere</u> during construction. You can go to school in Chadron, too.

DQ: I ain't goin' nowhere.

KEN: Just going to buy a tent and camp out? Whoops, you tore up your buy-a-tent money.

MOSS: You can have my money, DQ. We can camp out together.

KEN: Waitress, tell the kids the dance is over.

WAITRESS: Kids, the dance is over.

KEN: That's all the fun for today.

DQ: Well… what if Moss and me don't feel like goin'?

MOSS: Actually, we feel a lot like goin'. It's friggin' cold in here.

DQ: Sure… and anyway, I put to memory the maps and your simple-headed code.

(KEN *starts to slowly undress* WAITRESS. DQ *and* MOSS *are stunned.* WAITRESS *laughs, encourages* KEN, *who also laughs.*)

DQ: Who the hell wants to see old people screw?

(DQ *and* MOSS *exit.*)

Scene Eighteen

(*The living or sitting room of* O'GARR *and* CINTHIA. CINTHIA *is in an orange DOC—Department of Corrections—jumpsuit… dancing to an eighties country tune. A drink nearby, she is tipsy. A chair and a sofa are pushed back. After a few beats,* O'GARR *enters, sits down, drinks from a bottle of beer.*)

O'GARR: Burn that jumpsuit first chance you get.

CINTHIA: Fair and square, I won it.

O'GARR: Enough. Go change into something nice.

CINTHIA: If you're nice… (*She stops dancing, having just sloshed some of her drink out.*) …if you're real nice… Real nice and not on-the-fight… If you're real nice and say that this outfit becomes me…

O'GARR: It don't.

CINTHIA: Real nice boy with some special personal pleasure needs…

O'GARR: Christ.

CINTHIA: I – Earned – This! (*She performs a boozy fashion model runway strut.*) I – Am – A – Murderer. (*Pause.*) Murderess? Murderer sounds less feminine. And an ex con.

O'GARR: You ain't no murderer, Cinthia.

CINTHIA: Is Hooley dead?

O'GARR Self-defense.

CINTHIA: Baby's jealous.

O'GARR: Self-defense, Cinthia. You were detained and questioned. A minor episode of three hours.

CINTHIA: You're jealous. You're the rancher, the cowboy, the Man of the West. Sure. Yep. But I am the one who killed… with a gun. That makes me the… the Outlaw.

O'GARR: If it pleases you, Cin, to play this costume drama, fine. But that jumpsuit needs taking off and…

CINTHIA: Maybe later… after a few more drinkies. (*She starts dancing again, though this time with quasi seduction as motive.*) Um… baby, it feeellls sooo goooddd to be a genuine article… an outlaw… a Belle Starr kinda girrlll.

(*The doorbell rings.*)

O'GARR: Go change. I'll see who the fuck it is.

CINTHIA: (*Blocking* O'GARR.) I will answer the door, sweetheart.

O'GARR: Change outta that fucking stupid outfit.

CINTHIA: You're ashamed of me? (*The doorbell rings again.*) Jealous… jealous! Oh… you wanted to be the killer in the family.

(CINTHIA *swerves, dances around* O'GARR, *exits.* O'GARR *flops down into a chair, drinks from his beer bottle. After a beat or two,* FATHER BEN *enters, holding a couple of cheap travel bags. He is followed by* CINTHIA *and* DQ. *DQ is in jeans and a pull-over blouse and is dragging a heavy backpack.*)

FATHER BEN: (*Over-cheery.*) Hello the O'Garr house!

CINTHIA: O'Garr, we are now a full-fledged family! Here is our new daughter, DQ! (*She takes* FATHER BEN *by the arm.*) We'll be in church come Sunday… a real family with family values.

(CINTHIA *leads* FATHER BEN… *and they both exit.* O'GARR *and* DQ *look hard at each other for a few beats.*)

DQ: Bulldozers are comin' at dawn to Roches. (*Pause.*) Ken Adams owns a shitload of town now… or controls it.

O'GARR: Yep.

DQ: Won't be much left of my room… not after the bulldozin'. (*Pause.*) And there won't be room for me once the new motel and resort are up. Water workers, bottlers and such. They'll be takin' all the rooms… 'till somethin's built for 'em. Most of 'em'll be Meskins. Illegals. (*Pause.*) They'll be drillin' for water all over the county. Adams bought water rights all over. Adams says we're gonna have the largest bottlin' plant on the planet.

O'GARR: You want somethin' to drink?

DQ: A beer'd go good.

O'GARR: No.

DQ: No beer.

O'GARR: No beer.

DQ: Whiskey? (*Pause.*) Just havin' at you. But I do drink beer now and again.

O'GARR: No beer.

DQ: I ain't afraid of you.

O'GARR: If you got a thirst, drink ice water.

DQ: I never get that kind of thirst.

O'GARR: Then you ain't thirsty.

(CINTHIA *enters*.)

CINTHIA: We can't really be like your real parents, DQ.

DQ: That's to the good.

CINTHIA: But O'Garr and I… we're going to be the best mother and father a girl your age could ever want.

O'GARR: Cinthia, maybe we ought to talk. Let DQ drink some sweet, cold well water.

CINTHIA: We are havin' a talk right now, sweetheart.

DQ: I could wait outside.

CINTHIA: DQ, do not move… unless to a chair. (*Pause.*) O'Garr, you and I are going to adopt DQ.

O'GARR: Without warnin'… much less talk? No offense, DQ.

DQ: You don't need to do this, folks. Just let me have a place to stay. Maybe your bunkhouse? I can work. Gimme, say, $600 a month and found.

CINTHIA: I want you to be my daughter, DQ. O'Garr wants it this way, too, but he has not yet applied his brain to the concept. You, Mr. O'Garr, will love it.

DQ: Your bunkhouse would be nice.

CINTHIA: You can have the attic. We'll fix it up. It'll be whatever you want it to be.

(*The doorbell rings.*)

CINTHIA: Let's hold that thought.

(CINTHIA *exits.*)

DQ: (*Long pause as she watches him drink his beer.*) That Ken Adams has all the figures and angles. (*Pause.*) An entire planet going thirsty in just the next thirty to fifty years. Adams calls it <u>the privatization of water.</u> (*Pause.*) He's gonna be a millionaire for having scouted and fronted for that water corporation. And Ken Adams ain't the original cocksucker seein' to it that a big, goddamned-big straw gets plunged into underground lakes and oceans of good water. No, sir, there's Texas oilman T. Boone Pickens buyin' water rights. There's other corporations… takin' investment billions from A-rabs and New York poodle-fuckers. (*Pause.*) Me 'n Moss, we seen paperwork… when we broke into Adams' creepy silo. Investment companies, like Calvert, are throwin' big money at men like Adams. Why? Because there ain't no natural water in Las Vegas or Phoenix or El Paso. And soon enough, they ain't gonna be clean water… not for free least ways.

O'GARR: (*Hand up.*) Stop gibberin'. You're making my skull pound.

DQ: All's I'm sayin' is that we're on top of the Ogallala Aquifer.

O'GARR: DQ!

DQ: I'm tryin' to inform you, O'Garr. Las Vegas is already stealin' water from northern Nevada.

O'GARR: You better run for it when I count to three and stand up.

DQ: I don't run.

(CINTHIA *enters with* MOSS *who's in a new cowboy hat and boots.*)

CINTHIA: And here's Moss. He's going to make a fine hand.

(DQ *charges* MOSS, *gives him a passionate kiss.*)

O'GARR: Cin, what are you doin'?

CINTHIA: I am not <u>doing</u> anything. It is all done. And you did not have to participate. We are adopting DQ, no further discussion. I need this. Do not foul me up, O'Garr. (*To* DQ *and* MOSS.) You kids go on up to the attic. A brand new queen size bed is up there, just for the two of you. Kids!

(DQ *unwraps herself from* MOSS.)

CINTHIA: Take your bags upstairs. Settle in.

O'GARR: Hold on!

CINTHIA: You've been warned, O'Garr.

O'GARR: Those kids are not gonna fuck like chimpanzees up in my attic.

CINTHIA: Where would you like them to enact their love? On our front porch? In this living room? Be reasonable, O'Garr.

MOSS: You won't regret hirin' me, Mr. O'Garr.

O'GARR: Moss, you ain't hired on here.

CINTHIA: Yes, he is.

O'GARR: Moss now works for me?

CINTHIA: Yes. Moss cowboys for you.

O'GARR: My men do not live in the house. That's why my grandfather built that bunkhouse.

CINTHIA: Do we have to settle that right now? Everyone wants supper.

DQ: Me 'n Moss ain't hungry, thank you. (*Looks at* MOSS.) Guess we're just all tuckered out.

(CINTHIA *shepherds* DQ *and* MOSS *to an exit, with their bags, then returns to* O'GARR.)

CINTHIA: You findin' this new family... these new parental demands romantic?

O'GARR: Romantic? Yeah... romantic as a cold, rainy autumn and calves down with scours.

(CINTHIA *slinks to* O'GARR. *Back to audience, she begins to peel her orange DOC jumpsuit slowly down... holds it at her waist as* O'GARR *kisses...caresses her.*)

Scene Nineteen

(*Rubble from bulldozed buildings in the background, aluminum lawn furniture in the foreground,* LOUIE *and* ISABELLE *proudly walk back and forth. Champagne glasses and a bottle of champagne are on a rickety coffee table.* LOUIE *is tricked-out as Wyatt Earp and* ISABELLE *is in her Calamity Jane get-up.*)

LOUIE: This is how they promenaded in the Old West! (*Holds onto her. They cease walking.*) Isabelle, this is our moment. Our triumph. And we didn't have to do more than trust ol' Ken Adams.

ISABELLE: We trust him?

LOUIE: We got close tabs on Ken.

ISABELLE: We better. Our future rides on this.

LOUIE: (*Expansive.*) Our future. A new motel… a resort really… right here. A horseshoe-shaped, two-story paradise. Olympic size swimming pool.

ISABELLE: Every room a suite.

LOUIE: Glass, brass, and <u>chrome</u>… everywhere. A quiet bar. Three restaurants.

ISABELLE: Boutiques across the street. We'll have Paris couture.

LOUIE: A golf course.

ISABELLE: No more Hooley's General Store and Dry Goods.

LOUIE: No more keeping the Roche Motel together with baling twine.

(LOUIE *and* ISABELLE *resume their back and forth stroll.*)

LOUIE: And we didn't need the others. Fuck 'em.

ISABELLE: They thought they were too good for us. (*Pause.*) And O'Garr and Cinthia… they can just stay out of town.

LOUIE: Or they can spend money in town. (*Pause.*) Can't really hold a grudge, Isabelle, with folks who have no vision.

(KEN *enters with* WAITRESS. KEN *is in a white sports coat, dress shirt, creased jeans.* WAITRESS *is in a party dress.*)

WAITRESS: Ain't this all somethin'?

KEN: From rubble will rise a dream.

(*All four take to the aluminum lawn furniture chairs.* KEN *pours champagne into four glasses, distributes them.*)

KEN: A toast to our town!

LOUIE: A toast to the American West!

KEN: To the West… however tame and indoors it's gonna be.

ISABELLE: The champagne's flat.

WAITRESS: You always find something to bitch about.

KEN: Enough bickering. We're making progress. We are the beginning of the re-population of the rural High Plains. We are arresting atrophy. Be happy.

LOUIE: (*Sees someone.*) Christ, would you look at Aquinas!

(AQUINAS *enters, shambles in, stops, looks at the others. Living on-the-scout has given her a filthy, louse-ridden aspect.*)

ISABELLE: (*Softly… warily.*) Aquinas, where have you been? Everyone's been worried sick.

(AQUINAS *barks, yips, barks, growls, yip-howls, does what she images is a coyote dance. Then* AQUINAS *makes an odd motion with her hand, as if it is a paw and not a hand, waves goodbye… and exits.*)

Scene Twenty

(*At the bales,* FATHER BEN *is with* AQUINAS, *who appears worse-for-weather.* FATHER BEN *is in jeans and a golf shirt.*)

FATHER BEN: … but God *is* everywhere.

AQUINAS: (*Lifts a bale… looks under it.*) Not here. God is not here.

FATHER BEN: He is in all things. In the very air we take into our lungs.

AQUINAS: (*Arms outstretched, she spins around… stops.*) Am I slapping God yet?

FATHER BEN: Aquinas, I wish we could speak… of the same matters.

AQUINAS: I am too crazy for serious matters. Because…. Because I have been too filled with… filled all the way up… with "serious matters."

FATHER BEN: We are about to lose our water. Ken Adams has bought us, bought water rights all over the county. Bought them for a large water corporation that's going to bottle it.

AQUINAS: And the water shall hurricane within the bottles, gather itself in winds that roar one hundred and sixty miles per hour! All we have to do, Ben, is get everyone to do a water dance. We are, each of us, little more than water.

FATHER BEN: (*Pause.*) The High Plains will have no water for the lives that have been made here. (*Pause.*) What can I say to convince you to come with me?

AQUINAS: Because you think it's God's will?

FATHER BEN: Let's begin… begin walking… toward town.

AQUINAS: But I have been walking. Oh… what do you have to _do_ to convince me? Someone is always _doing_. The clouds are _doing_. The tiny bugs in the bales are most certainly _doing_. Hooley never stopped with his _doing_. (*Pause.*) Sweet, sweet Ben, what are you _doing_?

FATHER BEN: It'll be dark before long.

AQUINAS: And we shall have stars!

FATHER BEN: It's going to be a cold night.

AQUINAS: Cold. C is for Carnivore.

FATHER BEN: I can't leave you to a frigid night.

AQUINAS: Cold. O is for Opossum. They sometimes play dead. We can stay here and play dead. (*Pause.*) But then we wouldn't be the C in Cold. We wouldn't be carnivores, Ben, and that's not possible for humans, right? We are eaters of flesh. Even the flesh of Jesus.

FATHER BEN: Be reasonable, Aquinas.

AQUINAS: Cold. L is for Lime. Lime is used to cover dead humans someone doesn't want discovered as more than bones. Cold. And D is for Decumbent, which is to stretch out on the ground… or can mean to grow alongside the ground. There! We have spelled the word Cold.

(FATHER BEN *takes* AQUINAS *by the hand and attempts to lead her away, but she pulls away and laughs.*)

FATHER BEN: At least you find humor in our conflict.

AQUINAS: Conflict? I have no conflict with you. I did have conflict, but Hooley has passed away. What I do have is a skull full of freight that needs shipping to someone other than me.

(AQUINAS *darts in at* FATHER BEN, *kisses him, and darts away.*)

AQUINAS: If I were to define it, I would call that a mischief kiss.

FATHER BEN: Aquinas, give me your hand… trust me to lead us to town.

AQUINAS: (*Considers.*) I just remembered this: I never got a Lone Ranger mask when I was a girl. Why would a girl want a Lone Ranger mask? But I did. (*Pause.*) Ben, why don't you give me <u>your</u> hand?

(FATHER BEN *offers his hand and she takes it. Laughing, she tries to pull him down. He pulls his hand back, tries to offer it again, but* AQUINAS *now won't touch his hand.*)

FATHER BEN: I will order a Lone Ranger mask for you if you come with me.

AQUINAS: A young lady must not receive untoward gifts from a gentleman.

FATHER BEN: Aquinas, the sun will soon be down. I am afraid of rattlers.

AQUINAS: What if I am too crazy to be around people? What if you wake up beside me one morning and I am a bush of nettles?

FATHER BEN: You are not crazy!

AQUINAS: Why would you say such a thing? I <u>like</u> crazy.

(AQUINAS *raises her arms over her head… slowly extends them until her hands are over his head.*)

AQUINAS: Now I am a net. I am a net that's going to drop on you… a crazy net.

(AQUINAS *pulls her hands back at the last moment. His expectations evaporated,* FATHER BEN *falls on her with an embrace… kisses meant to be blessings as well as….*)

Scene Twenty-One

(*In the silo,* KEN *is up against a wall, legs stretched out, shot in the gut, a blood-soaked pillow held to his belly. Nearby are a couple of syringes.*)

KEN: (*Calling off stage.*) I was doing something good. Everybody was going to win. (*Pause.*) It's inevitable. You can't stop it. Killing won't stop it.

(O'GARR *enters, carrying a few DVD's.*)

O'GARR: You have more Westerns than I would a guessed.

KEN: Stop fucking around! I'm in pain.

O'GARR: If you was a film critic, would you say that *True Romance* is really a Western movie?

KEN: (*Peeks under the pillow at his wound.*) I miscalculated you. The others I read well, but you I did not anticipate… not at all. We hardly spoke. I thought you were staying out of it… keeping what you had. (*Pause.*) O'Garr, you weren't going to get much by water extraction.

O'GARR: What do you prefer, Ken? Early Tarantino or twenty-first century Westerns? (*No response.*) Easy question. You've seen all your discs, right?

KEN: Water bottling will help this town. Kids can leave high school and be able to stay in their hometown. That's employment. There'll be a new grocery store, a big, clean one, one that can support Aquinas for the rest of her life. The motel will have every amenity. (*Pause.*) You're just going to let me die?

O'GARR: That's a good guess, Ken. I <u>did</u> shoot you out there.

KEN: This can have a good ending.

O'GARR: That's what I want. A good ending.

KEN: Call 9-1-1. They can chopper me to a hospital.

O'GARR: I'd rather find a rope and hang you.

KEN: Is this about Waitress? Is that worse than my scouting for a water company?

O'GARR: Waitress?

KEN: She said you two had been in love.

O'GARR: Hanging, like from a tree out on these High Plains. That appeals to me. (*Pause*.) But I might be a lazy person, Ken, in which case… well, I'd let you die slow… by tomorrow at noon. (*Picks up a used syringe, flips it toward* KEN.) You ran out of pain juice. Nothin' more to inject. Hate to listen to you moan and scream for hours. And I can't run out on you. No man wants to die alone. (*Pause*.) You never answered my question. Modern Westerns or early-career Tarantino?

KEN: There must be something you want.

O'GARR: I'd argue that Dennis Hopper and a subtext that was a mix of Western 'n urban… but mostly Western.

KEN: I can write new reports. New reports to say the water around here won't pass health scrutiny. (*Pause*.) Name your price.

O'GARR: Sometimes there ain't a price.

KEN: Work with me, O'Garr, work with me on this.

O'GARR: Wrong thing to say, Ken. The only folks I've heard say, "Work with me," is car salesmen. You don't want to die, do you, with me thinking, at the end, that all I got done… was killin' a two-bit car salesman, do you?

KEN: I can do things for you, O'Garr.

O'GARR: No need. I'll forge enough documents… and sign off on your farewell letter.

KEN: I thought you were more man than for something like this. Taking me down with a hunting rifle while belly-down in grass! I thought you were better. More Western. (*Pause.*) You going to let that one pull of a trigger define you?

O'GARR: Maybe I am not one of those movie heroes. Like a gunfight out in the street. (*Pause.*) Give me one thing, Ken: you were not shot in the back. That I did not do. I shot you in the stomach. That's a round that goes in the front side. Funny… there's no exit wound.

KEN: Think!

O'GARR: I am thinking. I'm thinking on how I went off to university with a plan, a plan which did not work out. I went off to university to be a doctor, Ken. I went off with pre-med as my major. Yeah… I wanted to be a brain surgeon. (*Displays an ice pick.*) Tonight I am going to fulfill the ambition of my youth. I'm gonna be a brain surgeon. Ken, I 'm gonna perform a lobotomy on you… take this ice pick in through the corner of your eye. And I'm gonna scramble your brain… disorganize that front part of your brain that gets us all too much trouble from you. (*Pause.*) After I scramble your brain with this ice pick, Ken, I will, if you survive brain surgery… I will work on your belly.

(*Pause.*) I checked. We have plenty of antibiotics on hand. I'll do my best, Ken.

(O'GARR *starts towards* KEN *with the ice pick in hand.* KEN *rolls over, starts crawling, rolling, crawling, rolling and crawling… yelps and moans… rolls and crawls.*)

Scene Twenty-Two

(DQ *and* MOSS *are semi-waltzing real slow, real romantic.* DQ *is in a prom dress.* MOSS *is in clean cowboy clothes. Seated nearby are* AQUINAS *and* FATHER BEN… *in prom wear.* FATHER BEN *is attentive to* AQUINAS, *holds her hand. After a few beats,* CINTHIA *enters… in a sheath dress, holding a drink.* DQ *and* MOSS *waltz to an exit… and the music fades.* CINTHIA *sits near* AQUINAS *and* FATHER BEN.)

FATHER BEN: No sign of O'Garr yet.

CINTHIA: How 'bout that!

AQUINAS: O'Garr is taking care of us.

CINTHIA: Taking care of us? Wouldn't that require minimal concern for us first? (*Pause.*) DQ would like his approval on that dress. Do you think it's too poofy, Aquinas?

AQUINAS: Poofy? No, it's perfect.

CINTHIA: DQ wanted more cleavage. But I wouldn't buy her that dress.

FATHER BEN: This is so good of you, Cin, to have a practice prom at your home

AQUINAS: And to invite us.

FATHER BEN: Especially since… since…

CINTHIA: Bullshit. Once a priest, forever a priest.

FATHER BEN: Not quite. (*Pause.*) A pastor. Now I am a pastor. Non-denominational.

CINTHIA: I doubt God gives a hoot. And I sure don't. And that means O'Garr will keep attending church. So there!

AQUINAS: This is my first prom.

CINTHIA: And we'll take pictures later. We'll do prom poses. It'll be fun.

AQUINAS: Prom poses?

CINTHIA: The girl snuggles up to her prom date, but not too close.

AQUINAS: Not too close?

CINTHIA: Not too close, because girls don't want to have their hair spoiled or their flowers crushed.

AQUINAS: I like close. Don't I, Ben? Don't I like close?

FATHER BEN: Yes, we both like close.

AQUINAS: (*To* CINTHIA.) You like close?

CINTHIA: Close is real good. Close is the best… if the guy has showered off all the cowshit and sweat… and washed the Copenhagen out of his mouth.

AQUINAS: (*To* FATHER BEN.) How long before we get close tonight, Ben?

FATHER BEN: Well, Aquinas, we're at a prom right now.

AQUINAS: Later, Ben, after our prom… later, Ben, let's…. Oh, Ben, I love you.

(DQ *and* MOSS *enter, hand-in-hand.*)

DQ: I think everyone's ready for some of that fruit punch.

CINTHIA: Did you kids spike it? (*Silence.*) Oh, DQ, you spiked the punch with the last vodka bottle.

MOSS: Sorry.

(FATHER BEN *and* AQUINAS *stand.*)

FATHER BEN: Cin, this has been quite an evening.

CINTHIA: Oh, no, you're not leaving our practice prom.

AQUINAS: I want to get real close, Cinthia. I want to be so close that Ben is inside me.

CINTHIA: Ben, why not take a break for yourselves in our guest room? It's the one upstairs that does not have magazine pictures pasted onto its door.

FATHER BEN: We can wait.

AQUINAS: It's always better without waiting.

FATHER BEN: Thank you, Cin. Some things are better done in one's own home.

(FATHER BEN *and* AQUINAS *begin to walk away.* CINTHIA *follows along.*)

FATHER BEN: Give my thanks to O'Garr for straightening out the paperwork for Aquinas.

CINTHIA: You bet. The store will be rebuilt by spring.

AQUINAS: I do not want the store!

FATHER BEN: We have to have the store rebuilt… so that we can sell it. (*He embraces* AQUINAS.) We'll see you soon, Cinthia.

(FATHER BEN *and* AQUINAS *exit.* DQ *slips an arm around* CINTHIA, *hugs her, goes to* Moss.)

CINTHIA: Who wants spiked punch?

DQ: What about the prom pics?

CINTHIA: We can snap pictures of ourselves drunk once O'Garr gets home.

MOSS: I can't drink much. Got to ride fence all this week, what with fall comin' on… like before calving season.

CINTHIA: You got a day off tomorrow, Moss.

MOSS: Never got told any such by Mr. O'Garr.

DQ: Shut up and dance.

(CINTHIA *exits.* DQ *and* MOSS *slow dance.*)

Scene Twenty-Three

(*In the rubbled heart of town,* O'GARR *is seated on a metal lawn chair. He has a jacket on against an autumn evening's chill… with a county sheriff's badge on his chest. Nearby, tethered to a hitchin' post, is* KEN, *dressed in overalls with a covering sweatshirt.* KEN *is also wearing a harness with an attached leash… and he gives the distinct impression of having had his brain mangled.* LOUIE *enters after a beat, dressed against the cold.*)

LOUIE: Evenin', sheriff.

O'GARR: What's the latest?

LOUIE: (*Looks at an unresponsive* KEN.) Why keep bringing him around?

O'GARR: Get to the point: why are we meeting?

LOUIE: He's more a creature, a thing, than a person now.

O'GARR: Do I have to beat it out of you, Louie?

LOUIE: Well… Isabelle and me….

O'GARR: Short of money?

LOUIE: No, no, we're okay.

KEN: My name is Kenny.

LOUIE: Jesus suffering Christ.

KEN: I want to be a horseman.

O'GARR: It's cold out here, Louie. I got real fires to take care of.

LOUIE: Tell Ken to be quiet.

O'GARR: (*Looks over at* KEN.) Kenny's a good boy. Kenny's the best boy. (*To* LOUIE.) Have some decency, Louie. There but for the grace of God… ya know what I mean? Like what if it was you that tried to commit suicide… like in some complicated, slap-dash fucking manner?

LOUIE: He should be in a home.

O'GARR: Out here, on these High Plains, we take care of our own.

LOUIE: He is not one of us.

O'GARR: As one of us, Louie, as any man jack. He came into this country with a pioneering spirit. And you'd have Ken in some fucking home without sunlight, without fresh air, without the warmth of human companionship and concern? You ought to be ashamed, Louie, ashamed. One more word about Kenny boy and I will get out of this piece of shit chair and I will fuck you up.

LOUIE: I was only saying.

O'GARR: Spit out what you want.

LOUIE: Isabelle and me, we appreciate all you done for us. But as of right now, we're dependent on the payments you've arranged. Like children on allowances.

O'GARR: Until your new place is built.

LOUIE: That's what Isabelle is worried about. Instead of a motel, a motel like the one we had, you're havin' a Victorian bed 'n breakfast place built. We did say that we preferred a motel, right?

O'GARR: Bed 'n breakfast is better.

LOUIE: Don't seem so.

O'GARR: It will seem so later… by next summer.

LOUIE: (*Pause… looks over at* KEN.) But a motel is what we had. Not a bed 'n breakfast. How can we make big money with a bed 'n breakfast once the water bottling factory comes in? Tell me that.

O'GARR: Bottling factory? You still believe that shit?

LOUIE: They do own a slew of water rights.

O'GARR: Kenny boy, we gonna git ourselves a bottling operation?

KEN: Kenny's hungry.

(WAITRESS *enters, dressed for a chilly night. She waits.*)

O'GARR: Kenny ain't worried about a water extraction operation. Naw... a bed 'n breakfast is the way to go. With a name like... like Horseshoe Bed & Breakfast. Or.. The Lariat.

LOUIE: What if Isabelle and me... what if we don't like the new name?

O'GARR: We're finished talking.

LOUIE: (*Looks at* WAITRESS, *looks at* KEN, *looks at* O'GARR.) Well...

O'GARR: Louie, either go to your trailer, to Isabelle, and get warm... or take Kenny boy for a walk.

LOUIE: You're tellin' me to walk Ken?

O'GARR: I am offering you an alternative to gettin' warm at your place with Isabelle. You can walk the town with Ken… or go fucking home.

(LOUIE *looks back once at* KEN… *and exits.*)

WAITRESS: Hey, good lookin', what ya got cookin'?

O'GARR: I'm thinkin' your place… (*Pause.*) It's the itch I got right now.

WAITRESS: Why did we ever elect you county sheriff?

O'GARR: To keep the peace.

WAITRESS: You keep a lot of pieces around.

O'GARR: You're my favorite… always have been.

WAITRESS: (*Looks at* KEN.) Maybe I ought to take back up with Ken.

O'GARR: Sure. You two can fuck on Main Street. There's a money maker. Sell tickets. (*To* KEN.) Kenny boy, you want to fuck Waitress?

KEN: Ken is hungry.

WAITRESS: You got a filthy, heartless mind, O'Garr.

O'GARR: I like the inflection in your voice. Sounds like warmth comin' from a fresh-showered country girl.

WAITRESS: What about him?

O'GARR: We can feed him first.

WAITRESS: No… the mood in me don't want you right now.

O'GARR: That's a shame.

(WAITRESS *steps in front of* O'GARR, *offers her hand. With his hand in hers,* O'GARR *rises from the chair.* WAITRESS *lets go of* O'GARR, *goes to* KEN, *kisses his forehead.*)

WAITRESS: Poor, dear, kind Ken Adams… I wish you hadn't done to yourself what you done.

(O'GARR *and* WAITRESS *exit.* KEN *gives the moon a double-tone wolf-like howl… then another howl… and a howl as the stage goes dark in a black out.*)

End

www.ingramcontent.com/pod-product-compliance
Lightning Source LLC
LaVergne TN
LVHW051603070426
835507LV00021B/2737